# HANDS-ON

# STEAM

| Science | Technology | Engineering | Arts | Mathematics |

Nancy Balter

## Program Credits

Corinne Burton, M.A.Ed., *Publisher*
Emily R. Smith, M.A.Ed., *VP of Content Development*
Véronique Bos, *Creative Director*
Lynette Ordoñez, *Content Manager*
Melissa Laughlin, *Editor*
Jill Malcolm, *Graphic Designer*
David Slayton, *Assistant Editor*

**Image Credits:** p.140 Jill Malcolm; all other images Shutterstock and/or iStock

## Standards

NGSS Lead States. 2013. *Next Generation Science Standards: For States, By States*. Washington, DC: The National Academies Press.
© 2021 TESOL International Association
© 2021 Board of Regents of the University of Wisconsin System

A division of Teacher Created Materials
5482 Argosy Avenue
Huntington Beach, CA 92649
**www.tcmpub.com/shell-education**
ISBN 978-1-0876-6210-7
© 2022 Shell Educational Publishing, Inc.

# Table of Contents

# Research

## The Importance of STEAM Education

STEAM education is a powerful approach to learning that continues to gain momentum and support across the globe. STEAM is the integration of science, technology, engineering, the arts, and mathematics to design solutions for real-world problems. Students must learn how to question, explore, and analyze natural phenomena. With these skills in hand, students understand the complexity of available information and are empowered to become independent learners and problem solvers.

The content and practices of STEAM education are strong components of a balanced instructional approach, ensuring students are college- and career-ready. The application of STEAM practices in the classroom affords teachers opportunities to challenge students to apply new knowledge. Students of all ages can design and build structures, improve existing products, and test innovative solutions to real-world problems. STEAM instruction can be as simple as using recycled materials to design a habitat for caterpillars discovered on the playground and as challenging as designing a solution to provide clean water to developing countries. The possibilities are endless.

Blending arts principles with STEM disciplines prepares students to be problem solvers, creative collaborators, and thoughtful risk-takers. Even students who do not choose a career in a STEAM field will benefit because these skills can be translated into almost any career. Students who become STEAM proficient are prepared to answer complex questions, investigate global issues, and develop solutions for real-world challenges. Rodger W. Bybee (2013, 64) summarizes what is expected of students as they join the workforce:

> As literate adults, individuals should be competent to understand STEM-related global issues; recognize scientific from other nonscientific explanations; make reasonable arguments based on evidence; and, very important, fulfill their civic duties at the local, national, and global levels.

Likewise, STEAM helps students understand how concepts are connected as they gain proficiency in the Four Cs: creativity, collaboration, critical thinking, and communication.

# Research *(cont.)*

## Defining STEAM

STEAM is an integrated way of preparing students for the twenty-first century world. It places an emphasis on understanding science and mathematics while learning engineering skills. By including art, STEAM recognizes that the creative aspect of any project is integral to good design—whether designing an experiment or an object.

### Science

Any project or advancement builds on prior science knowledge. Science focuses on learning and applying specific content, cross-cutting concepts, and scientific practices that are relevant to the topic or project.

### Technology

This is what results from the application of scientific knowledge and engineering. It is something that is created to solve a problem or meet a need. Some people also include the *use* of technology in this category. That is, tools used by scientists and engineers to solve problems. In addition to computers and robots, technology can include nets used by marine biologists, anemometers used by meteorologists, computer software used by mathematicians, and so on.

### Engineering

This is the application of scientific knowledge to meet a need, solve a problem, or address phenomena. For example, engineers design bridges to withstand huge loads. Engineering is also used to understand phenomena, such as in designing a way to test a hypothesis. When problems arise, such as those due to earthquakes or rising sea levels, engineering is required to design solutions to the problems. On a smaller scale, a homeowner might want to find a solution to their basement flooding.

### Art

In this context, art equals creativity and creative problem-solving. For example, someone might want to test a hypothesis but be stumped as to how to set up the experiment. Perhaps you have a valuable painting. You think there is another valuable image below the first layer of paint on the canvas. You do not want to destroy the painting on top. A creative solution is needed. Art can also include a creative or beautiful design that solves a problem. For example, the Golden Gate Bridge is considered both an engineering marvel and a work of art.

### Mathematics

This is the application of mathematics to real-world problems. Often, this includes data analysis—such as collecting data, graphing it, analyzing the data, and then communicating that analysis. It may also include taking mathematical measurements in the pursuit of an answer. The idea is not to learn new math, but rather to apply it; however, some mathematics may need to be learned to solve the specific problem. Isaac Newton, for example, is famous for *inventing* calculus to help him solve problems in understanding gravity and motion.

# Research *(cont.)*

## The Engineering Design Process

The most essential component of STEAM education is the engineering design process. This process is an articulated approach to problem solving in which students are guided through the iterative process of solving problems and refining solutions to achieve the best possible outcomes. There are many different versions of the engineering design process, but they all have the same basic structure and goals. As explained in Appendix I of NGSS (2013), "At any stage, a problem-solver can redefine the problem or generate new solutions to replace an idea that just isn't working out."

Each unit in this resource presents students with a design challenge in an authentic and engaging context. The practice pages guide and support students through the engineering design process to solve problems or fulfill needs.

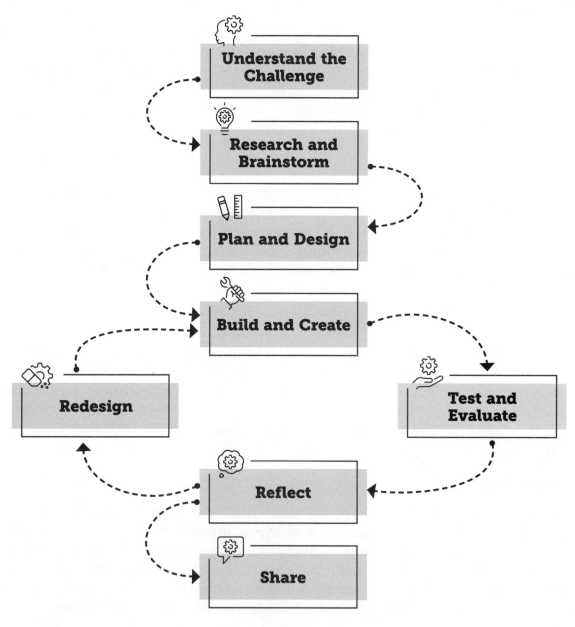

# Research *(cont.)*

## How to Facilitate Successful STEAM Challenges

There are some basic rules to remember as your students complete STEAM challenges.

### Both independent and collaborative work should be included.

Astronaut and inventor Ellen Ochoa is well-known for working a robotic arm in space. About that experience she said, "It's fun to work the robotic arm, in part because it's a team effort." She recognized that she was getting credit for something amazing that happened because of the collaborative work of hundreds of people.

Students need time to think through a project, both on their own and together with others. It is often best to encourage students to start by thinking independently. One student may think of a totally different solution than another student. Once they come together, students can merge aspects of each other's ideas to devise something even better.

### Failure is a step in the process.

During the process of trying to invent a useful light bulb, Thomas Edison famously said, "I have not failed. I've just found 10,000 ways that won't work." People are innovating when they are failing because it is a chance to try something new. The STEAM challenges in this book intentionally give students chances to improve their designs. Students should feel free to innovate as much as possible, especially the first time around. Then, they can build on what they learned and try again.

Some students get stuck thinking there is one right way. There are almost always multiple solutions to a problem. For example, attaching train cars together used to be very dangerous. In the late nineteenth century, different solutions to this problem were invented in England and the United States to make the process safer. Both solutions worked, and both were used! Encourage students to recognize that there are usually different ways to solve problems. Discuss the pros and cons of the various solutions that students generate.

# Research *(cont.)*

## How to Facilitate Successful STEAM Challenges *(cont.)*

### Getting inspiration from others is an option.

Students worry a lot about copying. It is important to remind them that all breakthroughs come on the shoulders of others. No one is working in a vacuum, and it is okay to get inspiration and ideas from others. It is also important to give credit to the people whose work and ideas inspired others. Students may see this as cheating, but they should be encouraged to see that they had a great enough idea that others recognized it and wanted to build on it.

### The struggle is real—and really important.

Most people do not like to fail. And it can be frustrating not to know what to do or what to try next. Lonnie Johnson, engineer and toy inventor, advises, "Persevere. That's what I always say to people. There's no easy route." Try to support students during this struggle, as amazing innovations can emerge from the process. Further, students feel great when they surprise themselves with success after thinking they were not going to succeed.

### Materials can inspire the process.

Students may be stumped about how they are going to build a boat…until you show them that they can use clay. A parachute is daunting, but a pile of tissue paper or plastic bags might suddenly make students feel like they have some direction. On the other hand, materials can also instantly send the mind in certain directions, without exploring other options. For this reason, consider carefully the point at which you want to show students the materials they can use. You might want them to brainstorm materials first. This might inspire you to offer materials you had not considered before.

### Some students or groups will need different types of support.

If possible, have students who need additional support manipulate materials, play with commercial solutions, or watch videos to get ideas. For students who need an additional challenge, consider ways to make the challenge more "real world" by adding additional realistic criteria. Or, encourage students to add their own criteria.

# How to Use This Resource

## Unit Structure Overview

This resource is organized into 12 units. Each three-week unit is organized in a consistent format for ease of use.

## Week 1: STEAM Content

| | |
|---|---|
| **Day 1**<br>**Learn Content** | Students read text, study visuals, and answer multiple-choice questions. |
| **Day 2**<br>**Learn Content** | Students read text, study visuals, and answer short-answer questions. |
| **Day 3**<br>**Explore Content** | Students engage in hands-on activities, such as scientific investigations, mini building challenges, and drawing and labeling diagrams. |
| **Day 4**<br>**Get Creative** | Students use their creativity, imaginations, and artistic abilities in activities such as drawing, creating fun designs, and doing science-related crafts. |
| **Day 5**<br>**Analyze Data** | Students analyze and/or create charts, tables, maps, and graphs. |

## Week 2: STEAM Challenge

| | |
|---|---|
| **Day 1**<br>**Understand the Challenge** | Students are introduced to the STEAM Challenge. They review the criteria and constraints for successful designs. |
| **Day 2**<br>**Research and Brainstorm** | Students conduct additional research, as needed, and brainstorm ideas for their designs. |
| **Day 3**<br>**Plan and Design** | Students plan and sketch their designs. |
| **Day 4**<br>**Build and Create** | Students use their materials to construct their designs. |
| **Day 5**<br>**Test and Evaluate** | Students conduct tests and/or evaluation to assess the effectiveness of their designs and how well they met the criteria of the challenge. |

## Week 3: STEAM Challenge Improvement

| | |
|---|---|
| **Day 1**<br>**Reflect** | Students answer questions to reflect on their first designs and make plans for how to improve their designs. |
| **Day 2**<br>**Redesign** | Students sketch new or modified designs. |
| **Day 3**<br>**Rebuild and Refine** | Students rebuild or adjust their designs. |
| **Day 4**<br>**Retest** | Students retest and evaluate their new designs. |
| **Day 5**<br>**Reflect and Share** | Students reflect on their experiences working through the engineering design process. They discuss and share their process and results with others. |

# How to Use This Resource *(cont.)*

## Pacing Options

This resource is flexibly designed and can be used in tandem with a core curriculum within a science, STEAM, or STEM block. It can also be used in makerspaces, after-school programs, summer school, or as enrichment activities at home. The following pacing options show suggestions for how to use this book.

### Option 1

This option shows how each unit can be completed in 15 days. This option requires approximately 10–20 minutes per day. Building days are flexible, and teachers may allow for additional time at their discretion.

|  | Day 1 | Day 2 | Day 3 | Day 4 | Day 5 |
|---|---|---|---|---|---|
| Week 1 | Learn Content | Learn Content | Explore Content | Get Creative | Analyze Data |
| Week 2 | Understand the Challenge | Research and Brainstorm | Plan and Design | Build and Create | Test and Evaluate |
| Week 3 | Reflect | Redesign | Rebuild and Refine | Retest | Reflect and Share |

### Option 2

This option shows how each unit can be completed in fewer than 15 days. This option requires approximately 45–60 minutes a day.

|  | Day 1 | Day 2 |
|---|---|---|
| Week 1 | Learn Content<br>Explore Content | Get Creative<br>Analyze Data |
| Week 2 | Understand the Challenge<br>Research and Brainstorm<br>Plan and Design | Build and Create<br>Test and Evaluate |
| Week 3 | Reflect<br>Redesign<br>Rebuild and Refine | Retest<br>Reflect and Share |

# How to Use This Resource *(cont.)*

## Teaching Support Pages

Each unit in this resource begins with two teaching support pages that provide instructional guidance.

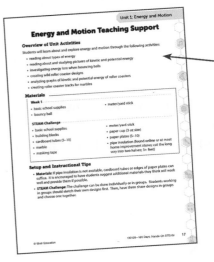

A clear overview of unit activities, weekly materials, safety notes, and setup tips helps teachers plan and prepare efficiently and with ease.

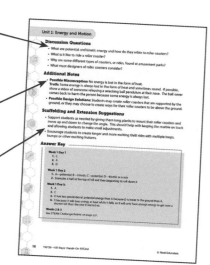

Discussion questions encourage students to verbalize their learning and connect it to their own lives.

Possible student misconceptions and design solutions further take the guesswork out of lesson planning.

Differentiation options offer ways to support and extend student learning.

## Materials

Due to the nature of engineering, the materials listed are often flexible. They may be substituted or added to, depending on what you have available. More material options require greater consideration by students and encourage more creative and critical thinking. Fewer material options can help narrow students' focus but may limit creativity. Adjust the materials provided to fit the needs of your students.

Approximate amounts of materials are included in each list. These amount suggestions are per group. Students are expected to have basic school supplies for each unit. These include paper, pencils, markers or crayons, glue, tape, and scissors.

# How to Use This Resource (cont.)

## Student Pages

Students begin each unit by learning about and exploring science-related content.

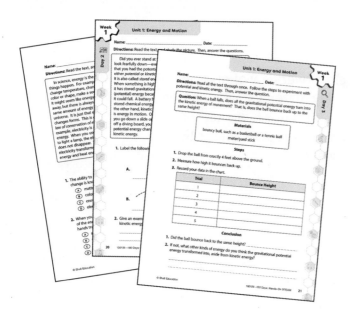

Activities in **Week 1** help build background science content knowledge relevant to the STEAM Challenge.

Creative activities encourage students to connect science and art.

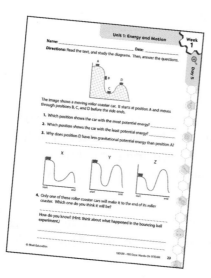

Graphs, charts, and maps guide students to make important mathematics and real-world connections.

# How to Use This Resource *(cont.)*

## Student Pages *(cont.)*

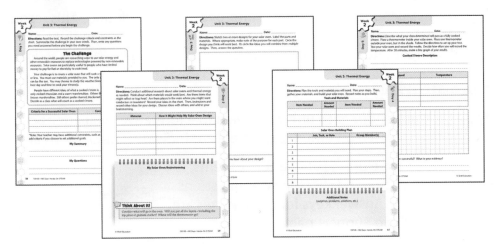

**Week 2** introduces students to the STEAM Challenge. Activities guide students through each step of the engineering design process. They provide guiding questions and space for students to record their plans, progress, results, and thinking.

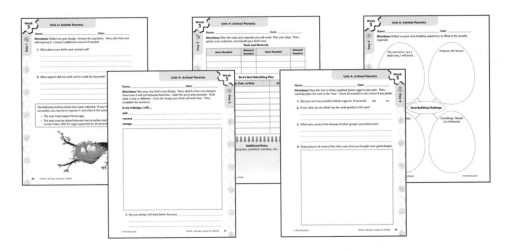

**Week 3** activities continue to lead students through the cycle of the engineering design process. Students are encouraged to think about and discuss ways to improve their designs based on their observations and experiences in Week 2.

## Quick Tip!

Staple all the student pages for each unit together, and distribute them as packets. This will allow students to easily refer to their learning as they complete the STEAM Challenges.

# How to Use This Resource *(cont.)*

## Assessment Options

Assessments guide instructional decisions and improve student learning. This resource offers balanced assessment opportunities. The assessments require students to think critically, respond to text-dependent questions, and utilize science and engineering practices.

## Progress Monitoring

There are key points throughout each unit when valuable formative evaluations can be made. These evaluations can be based on group, paired, and/or individual discussions and activities.

- **Week 1** activities provide opportunities for students to answer multiple-choice and short-answer questions related to the content. Answer keys for these pages are provided in the Teaching Support pages.

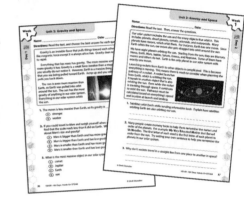

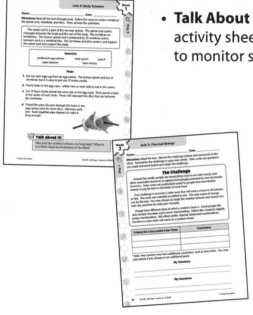

- **Talk About It!** graphics on student activity sheets offer opportunities to monitor student progress.

- **Week 2 Day 3: Plan and Design** is when students sketch their first designs. This is a great opportunity to assess how well students understand the STEAM challenge and what they plan to create. These should be reviewed before moving on to the Build and Create stages of the STEAM Challenges.

## Summative Assessment

A rubric for the STEAM Challenges is provided on page 221. It is important to note that whether students' final designs were successful is not the main goal of this assessment. It is a way to assess students' skills as they work through the engineering design process. Students assess themselves first. Teachers can add notes to the assessment.

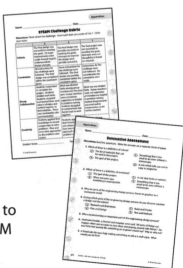

A short summative assessment is provided on page 222. This is meant to provide teachers with insight into how well students understand STEAM practices and the engineering design process.

# Standards Correlations

Shell Education is committed to producing educational materials that are research and standards based. To support this effort, this resource is correlated to the academic standards of all 50 states, the District of Columbia, the Department of Defense Dependent Schools, and the Canadian provinces. A correlation is also provided for key professional educational organizations.

To print a customized correlation report for your state, visit our website at **www.tcmpub.com/ administrators/correlations** and follow the online directions. If you require assistance in printing correlation reports, please contact the Customer Service Department at 1-800-858-7339.

## Standards Overview

The Every Student Succeeds Act (ESSA) mandates that all states adopt challenging academic standards that help students meet the goal of college and career readiness. While many states already adopted academic standards prior to ESSA, the act continues to hold states accountable for detailed and comprehensive standards. Standards are designed to focus instruction and guide adoption of curricula. They define the knowledge, skills, and content students should acquire at each level. Standards are also used to develop standardized tests to evaluate students' academic progress. State standards are used in the development of our resources, so educators can be assured they meet state academic requirements.

## Next Generation Science Standards

This set of national standards aims to incorporate science knowledge and process standards into a cohesive framework. The standards listed on page 16 describe the science content and processes presented throughout the lessons.

## TESOL and WIDA Standards

In this book, the following English language development standards are met: Standard 1: English language learners communicate for social and instructional purposes within the school setting. Standard 3: English language learners communicate information, ideas and concepts necessary for academic success in the content area of mathematics. Standard 4: English language learners communicate information, ideas and concepts necessary for academic success in the content area of science.

# Standards Correlations (cont.)

Each unit in this resource supports the following NGSS Scientific and Engineering Practices and Engineering Performance Expectations for 6–8.

| Scientific and Engineering Practices | Engineering Performance Expectations |
|---|---|
| Asking Questions and Defining Problems | Define the criteria and constraints of a design problem with sufficient precision to ensure a successful solution, taking into account relevant scientific principles and potential impacts on people and the natural environment that may limit possible solutions. |
| Developing and Using Models | |
| Planning and Carrying Out Investigations | |
| Analyzing and Interpreting Data | Evaluate competing design solutions using a systematic process to determine how well they meet the criteria and constraints of the problem. |
| Constructing Explanations and Designing Solutions | Analyze data from tests to determine similarities and differences among several design solutions to identify the best characteristics of each that can be combined into a new solution to better meet the criteria for success. |
| Engaging in Argument from Evidence | Develop a model to generate data for iterative testing and modification of a proposed object, tool, or process such that an optimal design can be achieved. |
| Obtaining, Evaluating, and Communicating Information | |

This chart shows how the units in this resource align to NGSS Disciplinary Core Ideas and Crosscutting Concepts:

| Unit | Disciplinary Core Idea | Crosscutting Concept |
|---|---|---|
| Energy and Motion | PS3.A: Definitions of Energy<br>PS3.B: Conservation of Energy and Energy Transfer | Scale, Proportion, and Quantity; Energy and Matter |
| Gravity and Space | PS2.B: Types of Interactions<br>ESS1.B: Earth and the Solar System | Scale, Proportion, and Quantity; Systems and System Models |
| Thermal Energy | PS3.A: Definitions of Energy | Energy and Matter |
| Animal Parents | LS1.B: Growth and Development of Organisms<br>LS1.C: Organization for Matter and Energy Flow in Organisms | Structure and Function |
| Body Systems | LS1.A: Structure and Function | Systems and System Models |
| Cells | LS1.A: Structure and Function | Systems and System Models |
| Plant Reproduction | LS1.B: Growth and Development of Organisms | Structure and Function |
| Air and Weather | ESS2.D: Weather and Climate | Cause and Effect |
| Earth's Materials | ESS2.A: Earth Materials and Systems<br>ESS1.C: The History of Planet Earth | Stability and Change |
| Ocean Currents | ESS2.D: Weather and Climate<br>ESS2.C: The Roles of Water in Earth's Surface Processes<br>ESS3.D: Global Climate Change | Systems and System Models |
| Plate Tectonics | ESS2.B: Plate Tectonics and Large-Scale System Interactions<br>ESS3.B: Natural Hazards | Cause and Effect; Patterns; Scale, Proportion, and Quantity |
| The Water Cycle | ESS2.C: The Roles of Water in Earth's Surface Processes | Energy and Matter |

# Energy and Motion Teaching Support

## Overview of Unit Activities

Students will learn about and explore energy and motion through the following activities:

- reading about types of energy
- reading about and studying pictures of kinetic and potential energy
- investigating energy loss when bouncing balls
- creating wild roller coaster designs
- analyzing graphs of kinetic and potential energy of roller coasters
- creating roller coaster tracks for marbles

## Materials Per Group

### Week 1

- basic school supplies
- bouncy ball

- meter/yard stick

### STEAM Challenge

- basic school supplies
- building blocks
- cardboard tubes (5–10)
- marble
- masking tape

- meter/yard stick
- paper cup (3 oz. size, 89 mL)
- paper plates (5–10)
- pipe insulation (found online or at most home improvement stores; cut the long way into two halves; 3+ feet, 1+ meter)

## Setup and Instructional Tips

- **Materials:** If pipe insulation is not available, cardboard tubes or edges of paper plates can suffice. It is encouraged to have students suggest additional materials they think will work well and provide them if possible.
- **STEAM Challenge:** The challenge can be done individually or in groups. Students working in groups should sketch their own designs first. Then, have them share designs in groups and choose one together.

# Unit 1: Energy and Motion

## Discussion Questions

- What are potential and kinetic energies and how do they relate to roller coasters?
- What is it like to ride a roller coaster?
- Why are some different types of coasters, or rides, found at amusement parks?
- What must designers of roller coasters consider?

## Additional Notes

- **Possible Misconception:** No energy is lost in the form of heat.
  **Truth:** Some energy is *always* lost in the form of heat and sometimes sound. If possible, show a video of someone releasing a wrecking ball pendulum at their nose. The ball never comes back to harm the person because some energy is always lost.
- **Possible Design Solutions:** Students may create roller coasters that are supported by the ground, or they may choose to create ways for their roller coasters to be above the ground.

## Scaffolding and Extension Suggestions

- Support students as needed by giving them long planks to mount their roller coasters and move up and down to change the angle. This should help with keeping the marble on track and allowing students to make small adjustments.
- Encourage students to create longer and more exciting thrill rides with multiple loops, bumps, or other exciting features.

## Answer Key

**Week 1 Day 1**
1. C
2. A
3. D

**Week 1 Day 2**
1. A—potential; B—kinetic; C—potential; D—kinetic or a mix
2. Example: a ball at the top of hill and then beginning to roll down it

**Week 1 Day 5:**
1. A
2. C
3. D has less gravitational potential energy than A because D is lower to the ground than A.
4. X because it will lose energy as heat while it falls, so it will only have enough energy to get over a shorter hill than the one it started on.

**Weeks 2 & 3**
See STEAM Challenge Rubric on page 221.

Name: _____ Date: _____

**Directions:** Read the text, and choose the best answer for each question.

In science, energy is the ability to do work. This means energy can make things happen. For example, energy can: make things move (or stop moving), change temperature, change color or shape, make a sound. It might seem like energy goes away, but there is always the same amount of energy in the universe. It is just that energy changes forms. This is called the *law of conservation of energy*. For example, electricity is a form of energy. When you use electricity to light a lamp, the electricity does not disappear. The electricity transforms into light energy and heat energy.

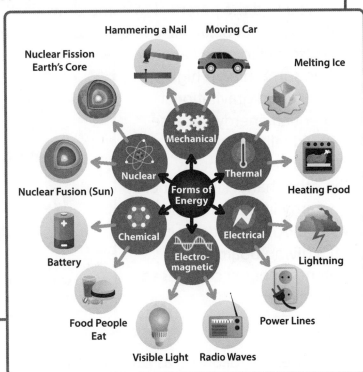

1. The ability to do work or cause change is known as _____.

   Ⓐ matter
   Ⓑ color
   Ⓒ energy
   Ⓓ electricity

2. When you clap your hands, some of the energy of the motion of your hands transforms into _____.

   Ⓐ sound
   Ⓑ color
   Ⓒ electricity
   Ⓓ light

3. What does the law of conservation of energy state?

   Ⓐ Energy cannot be destroyed.
   Ⓑ Energy cannot be created.
   Ⓒ Energy can change from one form to another.
   Ⓓ All the above.

Name: _____ Date: _____

**Directions:** Read the text, and study the diagram. Then, answer the questions.

Did you ever stand at the top of a diving board or playground slide and look fearfully down—even when you were little? That is because you knew that you had the potential to come down fast! Energy is often described as either *potential* or *kinetic* energy. Potential energy is work that *could* happen. It is also called *stored* energy. When something is high up, it has stored gravitational (potential) energy because it could fall. A battery has stored chemical energy. On the other hand, kinetic energy is energy in motion. Once you go down a slide or jump off a diving board, your potential energy changes to kinetic energy.

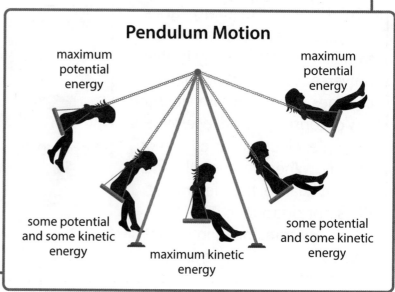

**Pendulum Motion**

maximum potential energy

maximum potential energy

some potential and some kinetic energy

some potential and some kinetic energy

maximum kinetic energy

1. Label the following as potential or kinetic energy.

A. 

_____

B.

_____

C.

_____

D.

_____

2. Give an example of something that has potential energy that changes into kinetic energy.

_____

_____

**Name:** _____ **Date:** _____

**Directions:** Read all the text through once. Follow the steps to experiment with potential and kinetic energy. Then, answer the question.

> **Question:** When a ball falls, does all the gravitational potential energy turn into the kinetic energy of movement? That is, does the ball bounce back up to the same height?

> **Materials**
>
> bouncy ball, such as a basketball or a tennis ball
> meter/yard stick

### Steps

1. Drop the ball from exactly 4 feet (1.2 m) above the ground.

2. Measure how high it bounces back up.

3. Record your data in the chart.

| Trial | Bounce Height |
|-------|---------------|
| 1 | |
| 2 | |
| 3 | |
| 4 | |
| 5 | |

### Conclusion

1. Did the ball bounce back to the same height? _____

2. If not, what other kinds of energy do you think the gravitational potential energy transformed into, aside from kinetic energy?

_____

_____

Name: _____ Date: _____

**Directions:** Roller coaster designers must consider potential and kinetic energy. Imagine you are a roller coaster engineer. You can design any kind of coaster that you want. What wacky things would the roller coaster do? Will it have sudden drops, multiple loops, tall heights, or crazy tunnels? Sketch your amazing coaster design. Write the name of your coaster on the sign.

**Name:** _____ **Date:** _____

**Directions:** Read the text, and study the diagrams. Then, answer the questions.

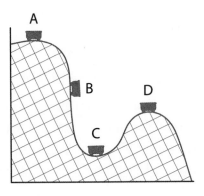

The image shows a moving roller coaster car. It starts at position A and moves through positions B, C, and D before the ride ends.

**1.** Which position shows the car with the most potential energy? _____

**2.** Which position shows the car with the least potential energy? _____

**3.** Why does position D have less gravitational potential energy than position A?

_____

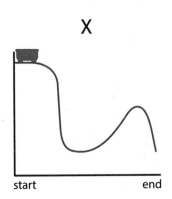

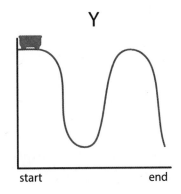

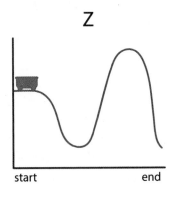

**4.** Only one of these roller coaster cars will make it to the end of its roller coaster. Which one do you think it will be?

_____

How do you know? (Hint: think about what happened in the bouncing ball experiment.)

_____

_____

## Unit 1: Energy and Motion

Name: _____  Date: _____

**Directions:** Read the text. Record the challenge criteria and constraints in the chart. Summarize the challenge in your own words. Then, write any questions you need answered before you begin the challenge.

# The Challenge

People love roller coasters. There are thousands around the world. Many engineers work on them to make sure they are safe and exciting. Roller coaster creators are always trying to create something faster, taller, or different to keep people coming back to the amusement park.

Your challenge is to create a roller coaster for a marble. The marble must successfully complete at least one loop-de-loop before its ride is over. When finished, the marble should end in a paper cup. The only source of energy can be gravitational potential energy. It can be supported by the ground, or you may choose to design a way to raise some or all of it up. You may use the materials provided to you, such as a marble, tape, paper cup, and some pipe insulation.

| Criteria for a Successful Marble Roller Coaster | Constraints |
|---|---|
|  |  |
|  |  |
|  |  |

*Note: Your teacher may have additional constraints, such as time limits. You may add criteria if you choose to set additional goals.

### My Summary

_____

_____

### My Questions

_____

_____

Name: _____ Date: _____

**Directions:** Conduct additional research about model roller coasters as needed. Answer the questions. Think about which materials would work best, and record your ideas in the chart. Then, brainstorm and record other notes or ideas for your design. Discuss ideas with others, and add to your brainstorming.

**1.** How could you ensure the marble stays on the track?

_____

_____

_____

**2.** How could you prevent the marble from slowing down?

_____

_____

| Material | How It Might Help My Roller Coaster Design |
|---|---|
|  |  |
|  |  |
|  |  |
|  |  |
|  |  |
|  |  |

**My Roller Coaster Brainstorming**

**Name:** _____ **Date:** _____

**Directions:** Sketch two or more designs for your roller coaster. Label the parts and materials. Where appropriate, make note of the purpose for each part. Circle the design you think will work best. Or circle the ideas you will combine from multiple designs. Then, answer the question and discuss it with your group.

**1.** What concerns do you have about your design?

_____

_____

Name: _____ Date: _____

**Directions:** Plan the tools and materials you will need. Plan your steps. Then, gather your materials, and build your roller coaster. Record notes as you build.

## Tools and Materials

| Item Needed | Amount Needed | Item Needed | Amount Needed |
|---|---|---|---|
|  |  |  |  |
|  |  |  |  |
|  |  |  |  |

## Roller Coaster Building Plan

|  | Job, Task, or Role | Group Member(s) |
|---|---|---|
| 1 |  |  |
| 2 |  |  |
| 3 |  |  |
| 4 |  |  |
| 5 |  |  |
| 6 |  |  |
| 7 |  |  |
| 8 |  |  |

## Additional Notes
(surprises, problems, solutions, etc.)

Name: _____ Date: _____

**Directions:** Test your roller coaster by placing a marble at the starting point and releasing it. Test the marble five times. In between each test, adjust the height of the starting point if needed. Record your observations for each test. Then, answer the questions.

| Height of Starting Point | Marble Completed the Track ✓ | Observations |
|---|---|---|
| | | |
| | | |
| | | |
| | | |
| | | |

1. Why is it important to run the test more than once?

_____

2. Would you consider your design a success? What is your evidence?

_____

_____

**Name:** _____ **Date:** _____

**Directions:** Reflect on your design, and answer the questions. Then, plan how you will improve it. Conduct additional research if needed.

1. Did your roller coaster work as you expected? Explain your answer.

_____

_____

_____

2. What aspects did not work well or could be improved?

_____

_____

_____

Draw a star next to one or more ways you will improve your design.

- My first design did not meet all the criteria because

_____

To improve it, I will _____

_____

- Add an additional fun element to the coaster (e.g., additional loop-de-loop, bump, tunnel).

- My own idea: _____

_____

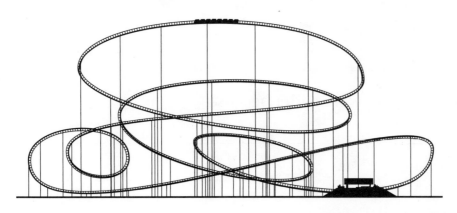

**Day 2**

## Unit 1: Energy and Motion

**Name:** _____ **Date:** _____

**Directions:** Plan your new roller coaster design. Then, sketch a few new designs. Label the parts and materials. Mark what is new or different, and circle the design you think will work best. Then, complete the sentence.

In my redesign, I will…

**add** _____

**remove** _____

**change** _____

**1.** My new design will work better because _____

_____

_____

Name: _____ Date: _____

**Directions:** Plan the tools and materials you will need. Plan your steps. Then, gather your materials, and rebuild your roller coaster.

## Tools and Materials

| Item Needed | Amount Needed | Item Needed | Amount Needed |
|---|---|---|---|
|  |  |  |  |
|  |  |  |  |
|  |  |  |  |

## Quick Tip!

Discuss with your group what you learned from your first build. Determine any changes or adjustments you need to make as a team.

## Roller Coaster Rebuilding Plan

|  | Job, Task, or Role | Group Member(s) |
|---|---|---|
| 1 |  |  |
| 2 |  |  |
| 3 |  |  |
| 4 |  |  |
| 5 |  |  |
| 6 |  |  |
| 7 |  |  |
| 8 |  |  |

## Unit 1: Energy and Motion

Name: _____ Date: _____

**Directions:** Test your redesigned roller coaster, and record the results. Then, answer the questions.

| Height of Starting Point | Marble Completed the Track ✓ | Observations |
|---|---|---|
|  |  |  |
|  |  |  |
|  |  |  |
|  |  |  |
|  |  |  |

1. What did you find was the best height from which to drop the marble?

_____

2. Were your planned improvements successful? Explain your evidence.

_____

_____

_____

**Name:** _____ **Date:** _____

**Directions:** Allow students from other groups to test out your roller coaster. Visit other groups' roller coasters and try them. Then, answer the questions.

**1.** Of the other roller coasters, which is your favorite and why?

_____

_____

_____

**2.** What about this challenge are you most proud of?

_____

_____

**3.** What would you do differently next time if you had more time and materials?

_____

_____

_____

_____

**4.** Draw a picture of yourself riding a full-sized version of your roller coaster.

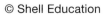

# Gravity and Space Support

## Overview of Unit Activities

Students will learn about and explore how gravity affects objects in space through the following activities:

- reading about gravity of objects in space
- reading about and studying pictures of our solar system
- experimenting with model moon craters
- modeling rocket paths from Earth to other planets
- analyzing distances of planets from the sun and making scale models
- creating products for a space museum gift shop

## Materials Per Group

### Week 1

- basic school supplies
- cake pan
- cocoa powder (enough to create a thin layer on top of flour)
- flour [enough to fill a 1-inch (2.5 cm) cake pan]
- rocks (3 small-sized)
- sieve or sifter

### STEAM Challenge

- basic school supplies
- beads (different sizes and colors)
- cardboard sheets (2)
- fabric
- foam sheets (3–4)
- modeling clay
- pipe cleaners (10+)
- posterboard
- shoebox
- string (3–4 feet, 1 m)
- various art supplies

## Setup and Instructional Tips

- **Materials:** This challenge is very open ended, as students will decide what type of product they create. Therefore, getting supply requests from students is encouraged. The materials listed are a starting point.
- **STEAM Challenge:** The challenge can be done individually or in groups. Students working in groups should sketch their own designs first. Then, have them share designs in groups and choose one together.

## Discussion Questions

- Should we continue to fund space travel? What does society gain?
- What types of traits and skills would be needed to be an astronaut that goes on long missions?
- What types of objects are in our solar system?
- How does gravity affect the movement of objects in our solar system?

## Additional Notes

- **Possible Misconception:** Mass and weight are the same thing.
  **Truth:** Mass is the amount of matter in an object. Weight is how much gravity is exerted on an object. This can change in different places. Astronauts weigh less in space but have the same mass.
- **Possible Design Solutions:** Students may create a variety of products, such as accessories, clothing, toys, games, puzzles, or home/garden decor.

## Scaffolding and Extension Suggestions

- Encourage students to spend time in the evening observing the night sky and have them share their experiences and/or write poems about space.
- Challenge students to create products that show objects in the solar system to scale (distances and/or sizes).

## Answer Key

**Week 1 Day 1**
1. B
2. D
3. D

**Week 1 Day 2**
1. Satellites are orbiting Earth. Earth is orbiting the sun. So as satellites orbit Earth, they also orbit the sun.
2. Answers should include mnemonics for remembering the order of the planets in our solar system.
3. Rockets do not travel in a straight line because their launch point is orbiting/moving, they are orbiting the sun (and sometimes other bodies) as they travel, and their destination point is orbiting/moving.

**Week 1 Day 5**
1. 30 inches plus the diameter of the student's sketched sun
2. Students should note that the inner planets are bunched close together and close to the sun, whereas the outer planets are spaced far apart.
3. Mercury, Venus, Earth, and Mars
4. Uranus and Neptune

**Weeks 2 & 3**
See STEAM Challenge Rubric on page 221.

**Day 1**

Name: _____ Date: _____

**Directions:** Read the text, and choose the best answer for each question.

Gravity is an invisible force that pulls things toward each other. It is kind of like magnetic force except it is always attractive. Gravity does not cause things to repel.

Everything that has mass has gravity. The more massive something is, the more gravity it has. Gravity is a weak force (weaker than a magnetic force), so you usually do not notice it. However, Earth is a massive thing, so you notice that you are being pulled toward Earth. Jump up and you will find that gravity pulls you back down.

The sun is even more massive than Earth, so Earth was pulled into orbit around the sun. The sun has the most gravity of anything in our solar system. Everything in our solar system orbits the sun.

1. The moon is less massive than Earth, so its gravity is _____ than Earth's.

   Ⓐ stronger

   Ⓑ weaker

2. If you could travel to Mars and weigh yourself when you arrived, you would find that the scale reads less than it did on Earth. What does this tell you about Mars's size and gravity?

   Ⓐ Mars is bigger than Earth and has more gravity.

   Ⓑ Mars is bigger than Earth and has less gravity.

   Ⓒ Mars is smaller than Earth and has more gravity.

   Ⓓ Mars is smaller than Earth and has less gravity.

3. What is the most massive object in our solar system?

   Ⓐ comet

   Ⓑ Jupiter

   Ⓒ Earth

   Ⓓ sun

**Name:** _____ **Date:** _____

**Directions:** Read the text. Then, answer the questions.

Our solar system includes the sun and the many objects that orbit it. This includes planets, dwarf planets, comets, asteroids, and meteoroids. Many planets have moons, which orbit them. For instance, Earth has one moon. Since Earth orbits the sun, our moon also gets dragged into orbit around the sun.

We have eight planets orbiting the sun. Starting from the sun, they are Mercury, Venus, Earth, Mars, Jupiter, Saturn, Uranus, and Neptune. Some of them have moons and others do not. Earth is the only planet in our solar system with exactly one moon.

Launching rockets from Earth to other objects is complicated. This is because everything is moving. This means there is much to consider when planning the pathway of a rocket. A rocket launches from Earth, which is orbiting the sun. It travels to another object that is also orbiting the sun. Even while the rocket is traveling through space, it continues to orbit the sun. Pathways must be calculated based on everything's speed and location at launch and landing.

1. Satellites orbit Earth while sending information back. Explain how satellites orbiting Earth are also orbiting our sun.

   _____

   _____

2. Many people create memory tricks to help them remember the names and order of the planets. For example: **M**y **V**ery **E**ducated **M**other **J**ust **S**erved **U**s **N**oodles. The first letter of each word is the first letter of each planet in order from the sun. Try writing your own sentence to help you remember the planets in our solar system.

   _____

3. Why don't rockets travel in a straight line from one place to another in space?

   _____

   _____

Name: _____ Date: _____

**Directions:** Read all the text through once. Study the image of craters on the moon. Then, follow the steps to make your own craters. Answer the questions.

The moon has gravity. Smaller rocks in space can be pulled toward it. Because the moon has very little atmosphere, fewer rocks completely burn up in its atmosphere. Instead, many rocks, called meteorites, hit the surface of the moon, creating craters.

**Question:** What can I tell about meteorite impacts from their craters?

### Materials

cake pan      cocoa powder      flour      sieve or sifter      three small rocks

### Steps

1. Spread an inch (2.5 cm) of flour over the entire bottom of the cake pan.

2. Put the cocoa powder into the strainer and tap it over the top of the flour until you have an even layer of cocoa over the flour.

3. Drop the first rock at a low height. Record your observations.

4. Drop the second rock from a higher height. Record your observations.

5. Drop, or gently toss, the third rock so it arrives at an angle into the pan, instead of straight down. Record your observations.

| Rock Impact | Observations (flour streak pattern, depth, where rock landed, etc.) |
|---|---|
| low height | |
| high height | |
| angled impact | |

## Talk About It!

Based on your data, what can you tell about craters? What similarities and differences did you observe?

**Name:** _____ **Date:** _____

**Directions:** Understanding travel in space means understanding that everything is rotating and revolving. Neither the point of departure nor your destination is ever staying in one place! Follow the steps to model this phenomenon.

### Steps

1. Working with a group, assign someone to represent the sun, Earth, a rocket, and another planet.

2. Create a sign to hold up, representing what you are: sun, Earth, rocket, or destination planet.

3. Act out the motions (rotations and revolutions) of each of these bodies, while the rocket travels from Earth to the other planet. Note that planets travel at different speeds from each other as they revolve around the sun.

Name: _____ Date: _____

**Directions:** Read the text, and study the chart. Then, complete the task, and answer the questions.

Data can sometimes be hard to visualize. In the case of space, distances tend to be incomprehensibly large. For this reason, scientists create scale models to help them see relationships. In this chart, the planet distances from the sun are listed in au (astronomical units). One au is equal to the distance from Earth to the sun (93 million miles).

| Planet | Distance from the Sun (in au) |
|--------|-------------------------------|
| Mercury | 0.39 |
| Venus | 0.72 |
| Earth | 1 |
| Mars | 1.52 |
| Jupiter | 5.2 |
| Saturn | 9.58 |
| Uranus | 19.20 |
| Neptune | 30.5 |

**Task:** Using the data above, create a scale model of the solar system. Use a scale of 1 inch = 1 au. Draw a sun at the far left and then use a ruler to measure the distances. Estimate where to put the dots the best you can. You will need to tape together a few sheets of paper to fit your scale model.

1. How long is your scale model in inches? _____

2. What is something that you notice about the solar system that you may not have realized before?

   _____

   _____

3. Which four planets are bunched closest together?

   _____        _____

   _____        _____

4. Which two consecutive planets are spaced farthest apart?

   _____        _____

**Name:** _____ **Date:** _____

**Directions:** Read the text. Record the challenge criteria and constraints in the chart. Summarize the challenge in your own words. Then, write any questions you need answered before you begin the challenge.

## The Challenge

Space museums are great places to learn about space. They often have exciting exhibits and interactive displays that help visitors grasp ideas and knowledge about space and the objects in it. When people leave such museums, they often like to buy things to take with them. For this challenge you have been asked to create a product to sell at the gift shop of a space museum.

You must make something for the gift shop that is an educational product that teaches or displays information about gravity and our solar system in some way. It must be something that customers can and want to use. You will decide who your target customer is and what the product will be. It could be a toy, game, book, item of clothing, accessory, piece of art, or another idea you can think of. You may use the materials provided to you.

| Criteria for a Successful Gift Shop Product | Constraints |
|---|---|
|  |  |
|  |  |
|  |  |

*Note: Your teacher may have additional constraints, such as time limits. You may add criteria if you choose to set additional goals.

### My Summary

_____

_____

### My Questions

_____

_____

Name: _____ Date: _____

**Directions:** Research the types of products that are found or sold by museums or zoos. Answer the questions. Then, draw or describe four examples of products that you found. Then, brainstorm and record other notes or ideas for your design. Discuss ideas with others, and add to your brainstorming. Conduct additional research about gravity and our solar system as needed for your product.

**1.** If you visited a museum, what types of products would you be most interested in getting from the gift shop?

_____

**2.** What types of products are you most interested in creating?

_____

_____

| Example 1 | Example 2 |
|---|---|
| | |
| **Example 3** | **Example 4** |
| | |

**My Gift Store Product Brainstorming**

**Name:** _____ **Date:** _____

**Directions:** Sketch two or more designs for your product. Label the parts and materials. Where appropriate, make note of the purpose for each part. Circle the design you think will work best. Or circle the ideas you will combine from multiple designs. Then, answer the question.

**1.** How would you describe your target customer (age, interests, etc.)?

_____

_____

## Unit 2: Gravity and Space

Name: _____  Date: _____

**Directions:** Plan the tools and materials you will need. Plan your steps. Then, gather your materials, and build your museum gift shop product. Record notes as you build.

### Tools and Materials

| Item Needed | Amount Needed | Item Needed | Amount Needed |
|---|---|---|---|
| | | | |
| | | | |
| | | | |

### Gift Shop Product Building Plan

| | Job, Task, or Role | Group Member(s) |
|---|---|---|
| 1 | | |
| 2 | | |
| 3 | | |
| 4 | | |
| 5 | | |
| 6 | | |
| 7 | | |
| 8 | | |

### Additional Notes
(surprises, problems, solutions, etc.)

Name: _____ Date: _____

**Directions:** Display your product for others. Answer questions about your design, and demonstrate how it is used. Ask them for feedback, and record what they say.

## Tell

**1.** Who is your target customer?

_____

_____

**2.** Describe the purpose of your product.

_____

_____

**3.** How does your product teach or share information about gravity and objects in our solar system?

_____

_____

## Show

**4.** Show how your product works or can be used. If possible, have others test or try it.

## Ask

**5.** What do you like about my gift shop product?

_____

_____

**6.** How can I make it better?

_____

_____

Day 1

Name: _____ Date: _____

**Directions:** Reflect on your design, and answer the questions. Then, plan how you will improve it. Conduct additional research if needed.

1. What about your museum gift shop product worked well?

_____

_____

_____

2. What aspects do you think need to change to better satisfy customers?

_____

_____

_____

Draw a star next to one or more ways you will improve your design.

- My first design did not meet all the criteria because

_____

  To improve it, I will _____

_____

- Create packaging that helps market your product.
- My own idea: _____

_____

Name: _____ Date: _____

**Directions:** Plan your new product design. Then, sketch a few new designs. Label the parts and materials. Mark what is new or different, and circle the design you think will work best. Then, complete the sentence.

**In my redesign, I will…**

**add** _____

**remove** _____

**change** _____

1. My new design will better satisfy customers because _____

_____

_____

Name: _____ Date: _____

**Directions:** Plan the tools and materials you will need. Plan your steps. Then, gather your materials, and rebuild your museum gift shop product.

### Tools and Materials

| Item Needed | Amount Needed | Item Needed | Amount Needed |
|---|---|---|---|
|  |  |  |  |
|  |  |  |  |
|  |  |  |  |

### Gift Shop Product Rebuilding Plan

|  | Job, Task, or Role | Group Member(s) |
|---|---|---|
| 1 |  |  |
| 2 |  |  |
| 3 |  |  |
| 4 |  |  |
| 5 |  |  |
| 6 |  |  |
| 7 |  |  |
| 8 |  |  |

### Additional Notes
(surprises, problems, solutions, etc.)

Name: _____ Date: _____

**Directions:** Display your improved product for others. Answer questions about your new design, and demonstrate how it is used. Ask them for feedback, and record what they say.

**Day 4**

### Tell

1. What change did you make to improve your product?

   _____

   _____

2. Describe the purpose and function of your product.

   _____

   _____

3. Why do you think your target customer will be more likely to purchase this product than your first design?

   _____

   _____

### Show

4. Show how your product works or can be used. If possible, have others test or try it.

### Ask

5. What do you like about the changes I made to my product?

   _____

   _____

6. How can I make it better?

   _____

   _____

**Day 5**

Name: _____ Date: _____

**Directions:** Answer the questions to reflect on the work you did for this challenge.

1. What would you price your product at? Why do you think that is an appropriate price?

   _____

   _____

   _____

2. What about this challenge are you most proud of?

   _____

   _____

3. What did you enjoy most about this challenge?

   _____

   _____

4. Draw a picture of people looking at your product in the gift shop of a space museum. Add thought bubbles or speech bubbles. Write a caption.

   _____

# Thermal Energy Teaching Support

## Overview of Unit Activities

Students will learn about and explore thermal energy through the following activities:

- reading about and studying pictures of thermal energy
- reading about and studying pictures of types of transfer
- experimenting with the conductivity of different colors of paper
- designing unique ovens
- analyzing a line graph of oven temperatures
- creating solar ovens

## Materials Per Group

### Week 1

- basic school supplies
- construction paper (black, white, and 3 others)
- drinking glasses (5)
- thermometers (5)
- water

### STEAM Challenge

- basic school supplies
- boxes (a few sizes to choose from if possible)
- construction paper (different colors)
- foil
- oven thermometers (2)
- packing peanuts (a few handfuls)
- paper plates (2–3)
- plastic wrap
- potholder
- s'more ingredients: graham crackers, chocolate, marshmallows
- tongs
- wooden skewers (5–10)

## Setup and Instructional Tips

- **Safety Note:** Items get very hot inside solar ovens. For example, students should use potholders to touch the metal oven thermometers. Parts of the s'mores may also be hot.
- **Week 1 Day 3:** This experiment requires a sunny day (or a heat lamp). It requires 1–2 hours for the cups to sit in the sun to absorb heat before making temperature readings.
- **STEAM Challenge:** The challenge can be done individually or in groups. Students working in groups should sketch their own designs first. Then, have them share designs in groups and choose one together.

## Discussion Questions

- What methods or technology do we use to increase and decrease heat?

- Why would people try to invent solar ovens? What are the pros and cons of solar ovens and solar technology in general?

- What are other things, besides ovens, that we use solar power for? Why?

- What are some ways people design shelter for warm or cold climates?

## Additional Notes

- **Possible Misconception:** Solar energy must be electricity produced from solar panels. **Truth:** That is one method. However, lots of things are naturally powered by solar energy. Plants are a good example. Be sure to discuss what solar-powered means with students.

- **Possible Design Solutions:** Students are likely to do internet searches and find ideas for solar ovens. Be prepared to respond to questions about whether they can use those ideas. Ask students not to copy other ideas exactly. Discuss the fact that engineers build on others' successful ideas, but make theirs unique somehow.

## Scaffolding and Extension Suggestions

- Students who need extra support should be encouraged to start by building a copy of another solar oven they find online. From there, they can see what works and tweak the project or start anew.

- Challenge students to measure the temperature of their oven and improve it to the point that its maximum interior heat is 50 degrees hotter.

## Answer Key

**Week 1 Day 1**
1. B
2. A
3. C

**Week 1 Day 2**
1. In traditional ovens, heat is transferred to the food through radiation. Some conduction also occurs when the racks heat up and transfer heat to the cooking dish and then to the food.
2. Plastic is an insulator. Wires are coated in it to protect people from the electricity moving through the wires.
3. gold—conductor, cotton—insulator, fabric—insulator, wood—insulator, foam—insulator

**Week 1 Day 5**
1. 250°F / 121 °C
2. 15 minutes
3. The temperature remained at 375 °F.

**Weeks 2 & 3**
See STEAM Challenge Rubric on page 221.

Name: _____ Date: _____

**Directions:** Read the text, and study the diagram. Then, choose the best answer for each question.

Heat is a form of energy, but cold is not. In fact, things get colder when heat energy leaves them. Heat always travels from warmer to cooler areas. When things heat up, the particles (tiny pieces) in them move faster. For example, the particles in a solid move a little bit. When heat is added and they melt into a liquid, the particles speed up, moving more. When more heat is added and they turn into a gas, the particles zoom around even more quickly.

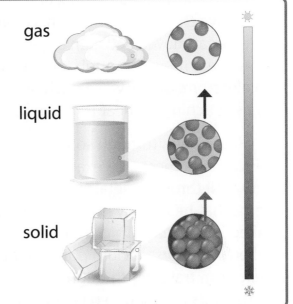

gas

liquid

solid

1. Heat is a form of _____.

   Ⓐ matter

   Ⓑ energy

   Ⓒ liquid

   Ⓓ cold

2. Something that is very hot _____.

   Ⓐ contains fast-moving particles

   Ⓑ contains slow-moving particles

3. Jayden made ice pops. He poured some lemonade in popsicle molds and then put them in the freezer overnight. The next day, the ice pops were frozen solid. What best describes what happened to the lemonade in the freezer?

   Ⓐ Cold from the freezer entered the lemonade, slowed down the particles and froze it into an ice pop.

   Ⓑ Cold from the freezer entered the lemonade, sped up the particles and froze it into an ice pop.

   Ⓒ Heat left the lemonade, causing the particles to slow down and froze it into an ice pop.

   Ⓓ Heat left the lemonade, causing the particles to speed up and froze it into an ice pop.

## Unit 3: Thermal Energy

Name: _____ Date: _____

**Directions:** Read the text, and study the diagram. Then, answer the questions.

Heat—also called thermal energy—moves from warmer to cooler places. It can move through conduction, convection, and radiation. Conduction happens when heat moves between objects that are touching. Convection happens when heat moves through moving liquids or gases. Radiation is heat moving as an electromagnetic wave, such as from the sun. Radiation does not need items to be touching for heat to move between them.

Heat moves through some things more easily than others. For example, heat moves very well through metal. Metal and other items that heat easily moves through are called *conductors*. Things that block heat are called *insulators*. A cloth potholder blocks heat from traveling through it. That is why potholders are used to pick up hot metal pots and prevent heat from traveling to your hands.

conduction

convection

radiation

1. When you warm your food in a regular (non-convection) oven, what kind of heat transfer do you think is going on—conduction, convection, or radiation? Explain your thinking.

_____

_____

2. Lots of things in your life make use of conductors and insulators. Wires, such as the ones on cell phone and computer chargers, are metal coated in plastic. Why do you think the wires are coated in plastic?

_____

_____

3. For each of the following items, write if you think they are a conductor or an insulator:

    (A) gold _____    (D) wood _____

    (B) cotton _____    (E) foam _____

    (C) fabric _____

Name: _____  Date: _____

**Directions:** Read all the text through once. Then, follow the steps to investigate heat absorption.

> **Question:** Which color of paper best absorbs the sun's heat?

> ### Materials
>
> drinking glasses     water     tape     thermometer
>
> construction paper in several colors

### Steps

1. Fill each glass with water.

2. Wrap each glass with a different color of paper. Leave one glass unwrapped for comparison.

3. Set each glass in the sun for one to two hours. Then, use the thermometer to check the water temperature in each glass.

| Paper Color | Water Temperature |
|---|---|
|  |  |
|  |  |
|  |  |
|  |  |
|  |  |

**Conclusion:** Based on your data, what color paper do you think best absorbs the sun's heat?

_____

Name: _____ Date: _____

**Directions:** Designing an oven or other home technology is not just about the engineering. People want their appliances to look good too. If you were to design a fancy or futuristic oven, what would it look like? Draw your oven in this kitchen.

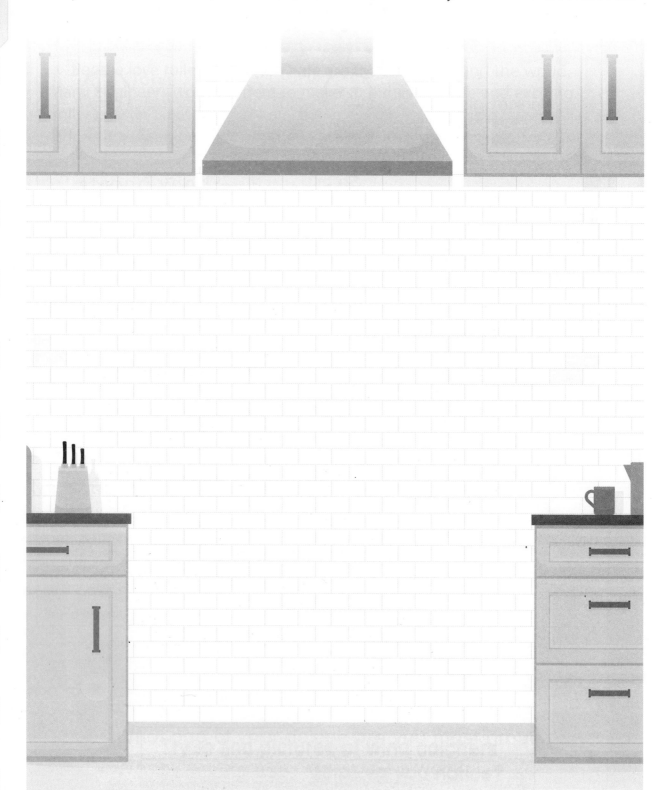

Name: _____ Date: _____

**Directions:** Read the text, and study the graph.  Then, answer the questions.

Maria was testing her oven.  She set it to 375 °F and then took the temperature every five minutes.  She graphed the information.

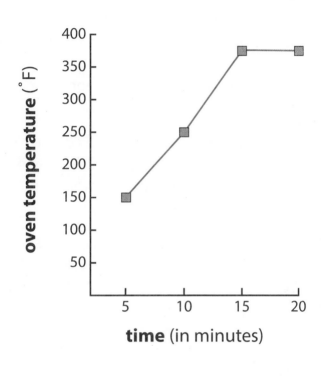

1. What was the temperature after 10 minutes?

_____

2. How many minutes did it take for the temperature to reach 375°?

_____

3. What happened to the oven temperature after 15 minutes?

_____

_____

Name: _____ Date: _____

**Directions:** Read the text. Record the challenge criteria and constraints in the chart. Summarize the challenge in your own words. Then, write any questions you need answered before you begin the challenge.

# The Challenge

Around the world, people are researching ways to use solar energy and other renewable resources to replace technologies powered by non-renewable resources. Solar ovens are particularly useful to people who have limited money to pay for fuel or electricity to cook food.

Your challenge is to create a solar oven that will cook a s'more in 30 minutes or less. You must use materials provided to you. The only source of energy can be the sun. You may choose to study the weather forecast and choose the best day and time to cook your s'more(s).

People have different ideas of what a cooked s'more is. Some people like only melted chocolate and a warm marshmallow. Others like a toasted, slightly brown marshmallow. Still others prefer charred, blackened marshmallows. Decide as a class what will count as a cooked s'more.

| Criteria for a Successful Solar Oven | Constraints |
|---|---|
|  |  |
|  |  |
|  |  |

*Note: Your teacher may have additional constraints, such as time limits. You may add criteria if you choose to set additional goals.

**My Summary**

_____

_____

**My Questions**

_____

_____

**Day 2**

Name: _____ Date: _____

**Directions:** Conduct additional research about solar ovens and thermal energy as needed. Think about which materials would work best. Are there items that might reflect or trap heat? Are there places in the oven where you might want conductors or insulators? Record your ideas in the chart. Then, brainstorm and record other ideas for your design. Discuss ideas with others, and add to your brainstorming.

| Material | How It Might Help My Solar Oven Design |
| --- | --- |
|  |  |
|  |  |
|  |  |
|  |  |
|  |  |
|  |  |

**My Solar Oven Brainstorming**

**Think About It!**

Consider what will go *in* the oven. Will you put all the layers—including the top piece of graham cracker? Where will the thermometer go?

**Name:** _____  **Date:** _____

**Directions:** Sketch two or more designs for your solar oven. Label the parts and materials. Where appropriate, make note of the purpose for each part. Circle the design you think will work best. Or circle the ideas you will combine from multiple designs. Then, answer the question.

1. What concerns do you have about your design?

_____

_____

Name: _____ Date: _____

**Directions:** Plan the tools and materials you will need. Plan your steps. Then, gather your materials, and build your solar oven. Record notes as you build.

## Tools and Materials

| Item Needed | Amount Needed | Item Needed | Amount Needed |
|---|---|---|---|
|  |  |  |  |
|  |  |  |  |
|  |  |  |  |

## Solar Oven Building Plan

|  | Job, Task, or Role | Group Member(s) |
|---|---|---|
| 1 |  |  |
| 2 |  |  |
| 3 |  |  |
| 4 |  |  |
| 5 |  |  |
| 6 |  |  |
| 7 |  |  |
| 8 |  |  |

## Additional Notes
(surprises, problems, solutions, etc.)

Name: _____ Date: _____

**Directions:** Describe what your class determined will pass as a fully cooked s'more. Place a thermometer inside your solar oven. Place one thermometer outside your oven, but in the shade. Follow the directions to set up your test. Test your solar oven and record the results. Decide how often you will record the temperature. After 30 minutes, make a line graph of your results.

### Cooked S'more Description

_____

_____

| Time Elapsed | Temperature |
|---|---|
| | |
| | |
| | |
| | |
| | |

1. Was your solar oven successful? What is your evidence?

_____

_____

**Name:** _____ **Date:** _____

**Directions:** Reflect on your design, and answer the questions. Then, plan how you will improve it. Conduct additional research if needed.

1. What about your solar oven worked well?

   _____

   _____

   _____

2. What ideas did you see from others that you might want to try?

   _____

   _____

   _____

Draw a star next to one or more ways you will improve your design.

- My first design did not meet all the criteria because

  _____

  To improve it, I will _____

  _____

- Increase the oven temperature by _____ degrees.
- Cook more than one s'more at a time.
- My own idea: _____

  _____

**Unit 3: Thermal Energy**

Name: _____ Date: _____

**Directions:** Plan your new solar oven design.  Then, sketch a few new designs.  Label the parts and materials.  Mark what is new or different, and circle the design you think will work best.  Then, complete the sentence.

**In my redesign, I will…**

**add** _____

**remove** _____

**change** _____

**1.** My new design will work better because _____

_____

_____

Name: _____ Date: _____

**Directions:** Plan the tools and materials you will need. Plan your steps. Then, gather your materials, and rebuild your solar oven.

### Tools and Materials

| Item Needed | Amount Needed | Item Needed | Amount Needed |
|---|---|---|---|
|  |  |  |  |
|  |  |  |  |
|  |  |  |  |

### Solar Oven Rebuilding Plan

|  | Job, Task, or Role | Group Member(s) |
|---|---|---|
| 1 |  |  |
| 2 |  |  |
| 3 |  |  |
| 4 |  |  |
| 5 |  |  |
| 6 |  |  |
| 7 |  |  |
| 8 |  |  |

**Additional Notes**
(surprises, problems, solutions, etc.)

**Day 4**

Name: _____ Date: _____

**Directions:** Repeat the steps to set up your test. Test your redesigned solar oven, and record the results. Then, answer the questions.

| Time Elapsed | Temperature |
|---|---|
|  |  |
|  |  |
|  |  |
|  |  |
|  |  |

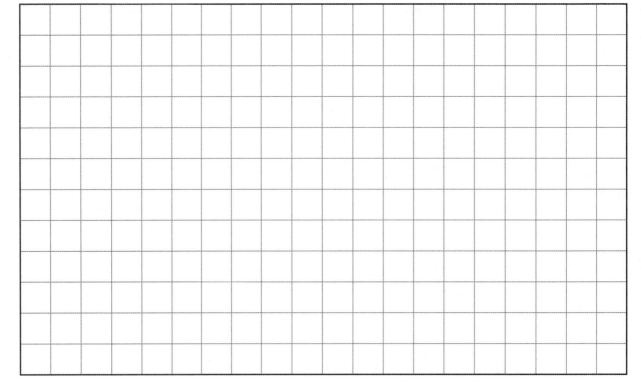

**1.** Did your new design perform better? What is your evidence?

_____

_____

_____

_____

**Name:** _____ **Date:** _____

**Directions:** Answer the questions to reflect on your solar oven.

1. What problems did you face, and how did you handle them?

   _____

   _____

   _____

2. What about this challenge was most difficult?

   _____

   _____

   _____

3. What would you do differently next time if you had more time and materials?

   _____

   _____

   _____

   _____

4. What advice would you give to someone who wants to make their own solar oven?

   _____

   _____

   _____

   _____

# Animal Parents Teaching Support

## Overview of Unit Activities

Students will learn about and explore how parents protect their young through the following activities:

- reading about organisms attracting mates
- reading about and studying pictures of how parents protect their young
- conducting mini research reports on animal behaviors for species survival
- design ways for birds to attract mates
- analyzing data on animal pregnancy and life span
- creating protective bird nests

## Materials Per Group

**Week 1**

- basic school supplies

**STEAM Challenge**

- basic school supplies
- cotton balls (10–20)
- craft feathers (10–20)
- dead leaves (handful)
- flower petals (handful)
- grass (handful)
- hay (handful)
- plastic eggs filled with jellybeans or marbles (2)

- recycled paper or cardboard scraps
- stalk-like plants (e.g., green onions, parsley)
- tongs (to pick up the nest)
- twigs (handful)
- optional for Week 3: PVC pipes and PVC elbows to create a V-shaped stand for students to balance their nests. (Alternatively, wooden dowels and duct tape can be used.)

## Setup and Instructional Tips

- **STEAM Challenge:** The challenge can be done individually or in groups. Students working in groups should sketch their own designs first. Then, have them share designs in groups and choose one together.

## Discussion Questions

- Why does every species have a drive to reproduce? What would happen if they did not?
- What are some ways that you have seen animals protect their young—whether in the wild, at the zoo, or even online or on TV?
- Many living things have hundreds or thousands of young—way more than can survive. Why would they do that?
- Why do you think some animals have elaborate mating rituals? What is the purpose?

## Additional Notes

- **Possible Misconception:** Strategies to reproduce work 100% of the time.
  **Truth:** These strategies do not always work. For example, the hard shells on nuts protect many seeds from predation, but there are some organisms that can get into the shells and consume the contents. Discuss this constant push-and-pull between organisms and their environments.

## Scaffolding and Extension Suggestions

- Support students as needed with their next construction by permitting them to use easier items, such as pipe cleaners to build their nests.
- Challenge students to limit their materials to three or four items.

## Answer Key

**Week 1 Day 1**
1. B
2. D
3. A

**Week 1 Day 2**
1. The species will go extinct unless it reproduces and makes sure that its young survive to reproduce.
2. By keeping the young in the middle of the herd, predators are scared away from attacking the young.
3. Example: Humans feed their young. They dress them in clothing appropriate for the weather. They take them to the doctor. They watch that they stay safe. They teach them things and help them to get exercise, so they grow strong.

**Week 1 Day 5**
1. 1
2. 65 years
3. 7
4. 1 year
5. Animals that have shorter life spans have more babies per pregnancy.
6. Answers may vary. Animals that do not live as long have more babies at a time to try to make sure that some survive. Animals that live longer tend to have fewer babies but care for them longer to make sure that they survive.

**Weeks 2 & 3**
See STEAM Challenge Rubric on page 221.

**Day 1**

Name: _____ Date: _____

**Directions:** Read the text, and study the pictures. Then, choose the best answer for each question.

Living things are constantly working to survive in their environment. They must find food, water, and shelter and escape predators. For the species to survive, they must also reproduce. Living things try to increase the chances that they will find mates. For example, fireflies produce light to attract mates of their own species. They signal back and forth to each other before mating. Male songbirds sing to attract female mates. Peacocks are famous for showing off their beautiful feathers to get the attention of peahens. Some birds will even do dances to attract mates.

**1.** Male songbirds sing to attract _____.

- (A) food
- (B) mates
- (C) rain
- (D) shelter

**2.** For a species to survive, members of the species must _____.

- (A) find food and water
- (B) find shelter
- (C) reproduce
- (D) all the above

**3.** How do fireflies attract mates?

- (A) with flashing light
- (B) with colorful feathers
- (C) with songs
- (D) with food and water

**Name:** _____ **Date:** _____

**Directions:** Read the text, and study the pictures. Then, answer the questions.

Once a living thing has reproduced, it becomes a parent. Parents work to keep their young alive. They have evolved all sorts of interesting ways to do so. For example, many birds build nests to keep their eggs away from predators. Some birds sit on their eggs for long periods of time to keep them warm and protected from harm. Male emperor penguins keep newly laid eggs warm by carrying them around on their feet.

A group of adult elephants will surround the babies in the herd to shield them from predators. Cheetah mothers move their cubs every few days to keep them hidden from hungry attackers. Many animal parents keep their babies physically close: kangaroos keep their young in pouches, orangutans carry their young around, and some alligators store their young in their mouths when danger is near.

1. Why is it important for a species to reproduce and work to make sure its young survive?

_____

_____

2. How do elephants help keep their young safe?

_____

_____

3. What are some ways that humans protect their young to make sure they survive until adulthood?

_____

_____

## Unit 4: Animal Parents

**Name:** _____ **Date:** _____

**Directions:** Choose an animal to do a mini research report on. Research your animal and find out how the parents of the species protect and care for their young. Find out if they have any interesting ways they attract mates. Make an educational poster in the space provided. Share it with others. Listen to others' reports to learn more. Note: Even if your animal does not stay with and care for the young when they are born, there are likely measures they take to ensure the survival of their young.

**How** _____ **Protect Their Young and Find Mates**

Name: _____  Date: _____

**Directions:** Birds have evolved all sorts of amazing characteristics to attract mates. Male frigatebirds have a red pouch under their beak that they inflate to attract females. Other bird species display beautiful feathers. Imagine you could design a bird with a wacky and wild way to attract a mate. What would it be? Draw a picture and describe what the bird does.

Name: _____ Date: _____

**Directions:** The chart lists a variety of mammals and shows the average number of babies each animal has per pregnancy.  It also tells the animal's average life span.  Study the chart.  Then, answer the questions.

| Animal | Average # of Babies per Pregnancy | Average Life Span (years) |
|---|---|---|
| elephant | 1 | 65 |
| orangutan | 1 | 40 |
| camel | 1 | 40 |
| panda | 2 | 20 |
| armadillo | 3 | 16 |
| tiger | 3 | 9 |
| prairie dog | 6 | 4 |
| rabbit | 6 | 2 |
| mouse | 7 | 1 |

1. How many babies does an elephant give birth to at the end of its pregnancy?

   _____

2. About how long does an elephant live? _____

3. How many babies does a mouse give birth to at the end of a pregnancy?

   _____

4. How long does a mouse live? _____

5. What trend do you notice about a mammal's life span in relation to how many babies it has per birth?

   _____

   _____

6. Why do you think some animals have few babies per pregnancy, whereas others have many?

   _____

   _____

Name: _____ Date: _____

**Directions:** Read the text. Record the challenge criteria and constraints in the chart. Summarize the challenge in your own words. Then, write any questions you need answered before you begin the challenge.

## The Challenge

One way some bird parents care for their young is by building nests. The eggs and hatchlings are protected from predators by being high off the ground. Nest building is not easy and requires some design to make sure the nest holds together and supports the growing bird family.

Your challenge is to build a bird's nest out of natural materials—no glue or tape allowed. When finished, it must be able to hold two small plastic eggs filled with jellybeans or marbles to give them weight. The nest will be tested by being lifted off the table with a pair of tongs. The tongs will not support the nest bottom. If the eggs stay in the nest for at least 10 seconds without falling out, then your nest is a success.

| Criteria for a Successful Bird's Nest | Constraints |
|---|---|
|  |  |
|  |  |
|  |  |

*Note: Your teacher may have additional constraints, such as time limits. You may add criteria if you choose to set additional goals.

### My Summary

_____

_____

_____

### My Questions

_____

_____

_____

Name: _____ Date: _____

**Directions:** Conduct additional research about bird nest designs as needed. Answer the questions based on your findings. Think about which materials would work best, and record your ideas in the chart. Then, brainstorm and record other notes or ideas for your design. Discuss ideas with others, and add to your brainstorming.

**1.** How are birds' nests constructed?

_____

_____

**2.** What materials do birds typically use?

_____

_____

| Material | How It Might Help My Bird's Nest Design |
|---|---|
|  |  |
|  |  |
|  |  |
|  |  |
|  |  |
|  |  |

**My Bird's Nest Brainstorming**

**Name:** _____ **Date:** _____

**Directions:** Sketch two or more designs for your bird's nest. Label the parts and materials. Where appropriate, make note of the purpose for each part. Circle the design you think will work best. Or circle the ideas you will combine from multiple designs. Then, answer the question.

**1.** What concerns do you have about your design?

_____

_____

## Unit 4: Animal Parents

**Name:** _____  **Date:** _____

**Directions:** Plan the tools and materials you will need.  Plan your steps.  Then, gather your materials, and build your bird's nest.  Record notes as you build.

### Tools and Materials

| Item Needed | Amount Needed | Item Needed | Amount Needed |
|---|---|---|---|
|  |  |  |  |
|  |  |  |  |
|  |  |  |  |

### Bird's Nest Building Plan

|  | Job, Task, or Role | Group Member(s) |
|---|---|---|
| 1 |  |  |
| 2 |  |  |
| 3 |  |  |
| 4 |  |  |
| 5 |  |  |
| 6 |  |  |
| 7 |  |  |
| 8 |  |  |

### Additional Notes
(surprises, problems, solutions, etc.)

**Name:** _____ **Date:** _____

**Directions:** Place the two weighted plastic eggs in your nest. Using tongs, pick up the nest from the side. Count 10 seconds or use a timer if you prefer. Answer the questions about results.

**1.** Did your nest successfully hold the eggs for 10 seconds?      yes          no

**2.** If not, what do you think was the weak point(s) in the nest?

_____

_____

**3.** What were some of the features of other groups' successful nests?

_____

_____

_____

**4.** Draw pictures of some of the other nests that you thought were good designs.

**Day 1**

Name: _____ Date: _____

**Directions:** Reflect on your design, and answer the questions. Then, plan how you will improve it. Conduct additional research if needed.

**1.** What about your bird's nest worked well?

_____

_____

_____

_____

**2.** What aspects did not work well or could be improved?

_____

_____

_____

_____

The following testing criteria have been adjusted. If your first design was not successful, you may try to improve it and retest it the same way you did before.

- The nest must support three eggs.
- The nest must be placed between two branches (real or manmade) and remain intact, with the eggs supported for 20 seconds.

Name: _____ Date: _____

**Directions:** Plan your new bird's nest design. Then, sketch a few new designs. Show how it will rest between branches. Label the parts and materials. Mark what is new or different, and circle the design you think will work best. Then, complete the sentence.

**In my redesign, I will…**

**add** _____

**remove** _____

**change** _____

**1.** My new design will work better because _____

_____

_____

## Unit 4: Animal Parents

**Name:** _____ **Date:** _____

**Directions:** Plan the tools and materials you will need.  Plan your steps.  Then, gather your materials, and rebuild your bird's nest.

### Tools and Materials

| Item Needed | Amount Needed | Item Needed | Amount Needed |
|---|---|---|---|
|  |  |  |  |
|  |  |  |  |
|  |  |  |  |

### Bird's Nest Rebuilding Plan

|  | Job, Task, or Role | Group Member(s) |
|---|---|---|
| 1 |  |  |
| 2 |  |  |
| 3 |  |  |
| 4 |  |  |
| 5 |  |  |
| 6 |  |  |
| 7 |  |  |
| 8 |  |  |

### Additional Notes
(surprises, problems, solutions, etc.)

**Name:** _____ **Date:** _____

**Directions:** Place the two or three weighted plastic eggs in your nest. Then, carefully place the nest in the "tree." Count 20 seconds or use a timer if you prefer.

1. Did your nest successfully hold the eggs for 20 seconds?      yes          no

2. If not, what do you think was the weak point(s) in the nest?

   _____

   _____

3. What were some of the features of other groups' successful nests?

   _____

   _____

   _____

4. Draw pictures of some of the other nests that you thought were good designs.

**Unit 4: Animal Parents**

Name: _____ Date: _____

**Directions:** Reflect on your nest-building experience by completing the graphic organizer.

The next time I see a bird's nest, I will think...

Problems We Solved

**Nest-Building Challenge**

My Favorite Part

Something I Would Do Differently

© Shell Education

# Body Systems Teaching Support

## Overview of Unit Activities

Students will learn about and explore body systems through the following activities:

- reading about organs and tissues
- reading about and studying pictures of body systems
- building models of human spines
- creating pasta skeletons
- analyzing a graph of exercise pulse rate data
- creating protective structures for eggs (delicate organs)

## Materials Per Group

### Week 1

- basic school supplies
- cardboard egg carton
- foam
- hole punch
- pipe cleaners (3)

### STEAM Challenge

- balloons (2)
- basic school supplies
- bubble wrap
- dried pasta (different shapes)
- egg cartons (2)
- fabric
- plastic wrap
- shoebox
- splatter mat, such as trash bags
- straws (5–10)
- uncooked eggs (2)
- yarn (3–4 feet, 1 m)

## Setup and Instructional Tips

- **Safety Note:** Keep students a safe distance away when items are being dropped. Make sure they are not dropping sharp objects or anything hazardous. Safety goggles are recommended during the drops.
- **STEAM Challenge:** The challenge can be done individually or in groups. Students working in groups should sketch their own designs first. Then, have them share designs in groups and choose one together.
- **Testing Days:** Set up a splatter mat, such as trash bags, to protect the floor where the egg containers and eggs will fall.

## Discussion Questions

- What are some ways that we have control over keeping our body systems healthy?
- If you could create another body system, what would it do and how would it help the body function?
- What would be the pros and cons of being a doctor or a vet?
- Do you think some of the body's systems are more important than others? If so, which one(s) and why? If not, why?

## Additional Notes

- **Possible Misconception:** Body systems work independently of each other.
  **Truth:** The body's organ systems are interconnected and depend on each other to function.
- **Possible Design Solutions:** Students will create various protective structures around their eggs, possibly mimicking the skeletal system.

## Scaffolding and Extension Suggestions

- Support students as needed by having them start by dropping practice items from lower heights.
- Challenge students to create structures to protect two eggs together.

## Answer Key

**Week 1 Day 1**
1. A
2. C
3. C, E, G

**Week 1 Day 2**
1. Example: Many muscles are attached to bones, and they work together to move the body.
2. Example: The heart is a muscle and so might be considered to be part of the muscular (or musculoskeletal) systems.

**Week 1 Day 5**
1. 40 bpm
2. 1:03 p.m.; her pulse (heart) rate started to increase
3. 150 bpm
4. 60 bpm

**Weeks 2 & 3**
See STEAM Challenge Rubric on page 221.

Name: _____ Date: _____

**Directions:** Read the text, and choose the best answer for each question.

Some living things are one single cell. If you looked at a drop of pond water under a microscope, you might see a bunch of different single-celled living things. Most of the living things you know of—cats, dogs, humans, flies, flowers—are made of billions of cells. They are called multicellular living things. These life forms are a terrific example of teamwork. Different kinds of cells work together. For example, your body is made up of skin cells, lung cells, brain cells, stomach cells, and more.

A group of the same type of cells working together is called tissue. Touch your face or the surface of your arm, and you are touching skin tissue. Different tissues work together to make up organs. Your skin is an organ. It not only has skin tissue but also blood vessel tissue to bring it oxygen, nerve tissue that gives you your sense of touch, and more. You have lots of organs in your body, including your lungs, heart, stomach, kidneys, and brain.

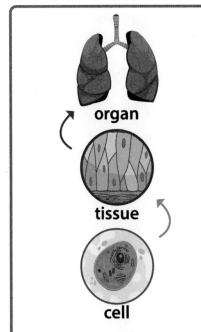

organ

tissue

cell

Lung cells make up lung tissue. Lung tissue plus other types of tissue combine to make up a lung.

1. Which of these is in order from least to greatest level or organization?

   (A) cells, tissues, organ

   (B) cells, organ, tissues

   (C) tissues, cells, organ

   (D) tissues, organ, cells

2. Which of the following is defined as *two or more types of tissue working together to do something*?

   (A) cell

   (B) tissue

   (C) organ

   (D) membrane

3. Which of the following is NOT an *organ* of the human body? You may select multiple answers.

   (A) brain

   (B) lung

   (C) egg

   (D) skin

   (E) blood cell

   (F) stomach

   (G) brain cell

**Day 2**

Name: _____ Date: _____

**Directions:** Read the text, and study the chart. Then, answer the questions.

Your organs and tissues work together to make up your body systems. Some organs are part of more than one system.

| Body System | | Major Parts | Function |
|---|---|---|---|
| circulatory | | heart, blood, blood vessels | brings oxygen and nutrients to cells and takes away waste |
| digestive | | mouth, esophagus, liver, stomach, small intestine, large intestine | turns food into energy that the body can use |
| respiratory | | nose, mouth, throat, voice box, windpipe (trachea), lungs | moves air into your body and takes out waste gases |
| muscular | | muscles | allows the body to move and pushes blood and food through the body |
| nervous | | brain, spinal cord, nerves | takes in information through the senses and acts as a central command for the entire body |

1. The muscular system is sometimes called the musculoskeletal system. Why might the muscles and skeleton be considered one system?

_____

_____

2. The heart is part of the circulatory system. Are there other systems that the heart is also part of? Explain your reasoning.

_____

_____

Name: _____  Date: _____

**Directions:** Read all the text through once. Follow the steps to create a model of the spinal cord, vertebrae, and discs. Then, answer the questions.

The spinal cord is a part of the nervous system. The spinal cord carries messages between the brain and the rest of the body. The vertebrae are backbones. The human spinal cord is protected by 33 vertebrae and in between each is a vertebral disc. The vertebrae and discs protect and support the spinal cord and support the body.

### Materials

cardboard egg cartons          foam sheets          pencil

pipe cleaners                              hole punch

### Steps

1. Cut out each egg cup from an egg carton. The human spinal cord has 33 vertebrae, but it is okay to just use 12 in this model.

2. Punch holes in the egg cups—either two on each side or one in the center.

3. Cut 12 foam circles (about the same size as the egg cups). Then, punch a hole in the center of each circle. These will represent the discs that are between the vertebrae.

4. Thread the pipe cleaners through the holes in the egg cartons and the foam discs. Alternate each one. Twist together pipe cleaners to make it long enough.

 **Talk About It!**

Why isn't the vertebral column one long bone? What do you think might be the purpose of the discs?

## Unit 5: Body Systems

**Name:** _____ **Date:** _____

**Directions:** Some people study *comparative anatomy*. They compare the body structures of different living things. Imagine you are comparing the skeletal systems of a human and a dog. Glue different shapes of pasta on paper to create models of a human and a dog skeleton. Then, label some of the pasta "bones" that you notice that are similar.

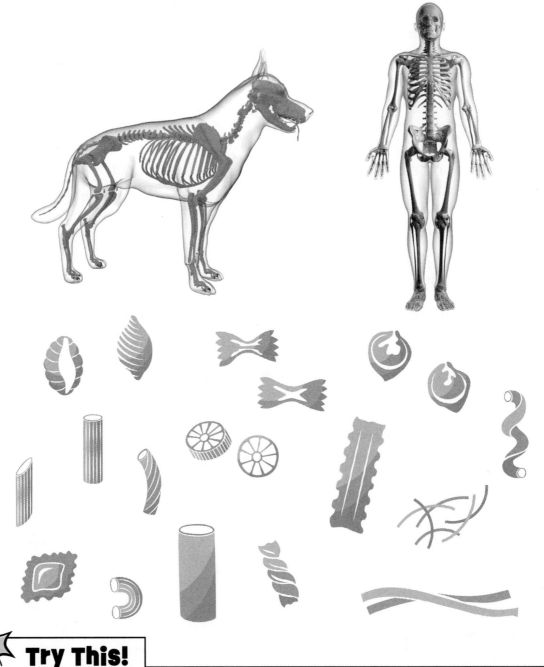

### Try This!

Choose a different animal. Do some research to discover what its skeleton looks like. Make it with pasta, too!

Name: _____ Date: _____

**Directions:** Read the text, and study the graph. Then, answer the questions.

Stair walking is an aerobic activity, which means it works the heart. Maria spent a few minutes walking up and down the stairs. She monitored her heart rate by measuring her pulse. The pulse rate increased as her heartbeat increased. She started by stretching at 1:00 p.m. Immediately after stretching, she started climbing stairs. Then, she spent a few minutes cooling down. She graphed her pulse rate from the time she began stretching until she finished her cool down.

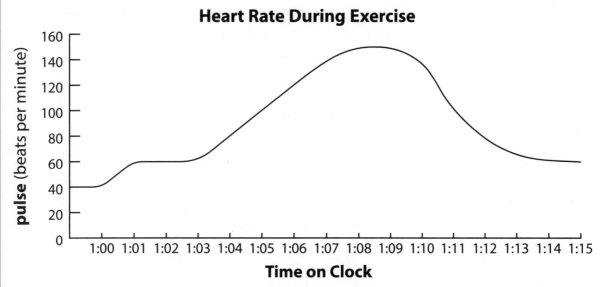

**Heart Rate During Exercise**

1. Maria was resting before she started stretching at 1:00 p.m. According to the graph, what is Maria's resting pulse? _____

2. What time did Maria finish stretching and start walking the stairs? Explain the reasoning for your answer.

   _____

   _____

3. What was Maria's maximum heart (pulse) rate during this time period?

   _____

4. What was Maria's pulse at 1:15 p.m.? _____

Name: _____  Date: _____

**Directions:** Read the text. Record the challenge criteria and constraints in the chart. Summarize the challenge in your own words. Then, write any questions you need answered before you begin the challenge.

# The Challenge

The human skeleton helps protect vital organs. Studying these structures can help when doctors need to repair fractured skulls and ribs. It can also help us think about how to create protection for other fragile items.

Imagine that an uncooked egg is a brain. Your challenge is to design a structure to protect your "egg brain" so it survives a fall from the top of a one-story building (about 14 feet, or 4.3 m).

You may use materials provided to you. You may not use liquids or glass. The structure must be your group's unique invention. The maximum size of your finished structure cannot exceed 2 feet (61 cm) in any direction. The maximum weight cannot exceed 5 pounds (2.3 kg). When the structure is released, everything must fall together. No holding string, chutes, elastic, etc.

| Criteria for a Successful Egg Brain Case | Constraints |
|---|---|
|  |  |
|  |  |
|  |  |

*Note: Your teacher may have additional constraints, such as time limits. You may add criteria if you choose to set additional goals.

## My Summary

_____

_____

## My Questions

_____

_____

Name: _____ Date: _____

**Directions:** Do some research to see what natural protection the body has for the heart, lungs, and brain so that they are more likely to survive impact. Answer the question. Think about which materials would work best, and record your ideas in the chart. Then, brainstorm and record other notes or ideas for your design. Discuss ideas with others, and add to your brainstorming.

1. What ideas or important information did you learn from your research?

_____

_____

| Material | How It Might Function or Protect the Egg |
|---|---|
|  |  |
|  |  |
|  |  |
|  |  |
|  |  |
|  |  |

**My Egg Brain Case Brainstorming**

Name: _____ Date: _____

**Directions:** Sketch two or more designs for your egg brain case. Label the parts and materials. Where appropriate, make note of the purpose for each part. Circle the design you think will work best. Or circle the ideas you will combine from multiple designs. Then, answer the question and discuss it with your group.

**1.** What concerns do you have about your design?

_____

_____

**Name:** _____ **Date:** _____

**Directions:** Plan the tools and materials you will need. Plan your steps. Then, gather your materials, and build your egg brain case. Record notes as you build.

### Tools and Materials

| Item Needed | Amount Needed | Item Needed | Amount Needed |
|---|---|---|---|
|  |  |  |  |
|  |  |  |  |
|  |  |  |  |

### Egg Brain Case Building Plan

|  | Job, Task, or Role | Group Member(s) |
|---|---|---|
| 1 |  |  |
| 2 |  |  |
| 3 |  |  |
| 4 |  |  |
| 5 |  |  |
| 6 |  |  |
| 7 |  |  |
| 8 |  |  |

### Additional Notes
(surprises, problems, solutions, etc.)

## Unit 5: Body Systems

**Name:** _____ **Date:** _____

**Directions:** Nestle your egg in its egg brain case and drop it from a height of one story, or about 14 feet (4.3 m). Observe and record the results. Then, answer the questions.

**Egg After Drop**

1. Describe the condition of the egg after the drop.

   _____

   _____

2. Describe the condition of the case after the drop.

   _____

   _____

3. Would you consider your design successful? Explain your evidence.

   _____

   _____

   _____

Name: _____ Date: _____

**Directions:** Reflect on your design, and answer the questions. Then, plan how you will improve it. Conduct additional research if needed.

1. What about your egg brain case worked well?

_____

_____

_____

2. What ideas did you see from other groups that you might want to try?

_____

_____

_____

Draw a star next to one or more ways you will improve your design.

- My first design did not meet all the criteria because

_____

To improve it, I will _____

_____

- Drop the egg from a greater height (with teacher approval).
- Create a case to protect two eggs.
- My own idea: _____

_____

**Day 2**

Name: _____ Date: _____

**Directions:** Plan your new egg brain case design. Then, sketch a few new designs. Label the parts and materials. Mark what is new or different, and circle the design you think will work best. Then, complete the sentence.

**In my redesign, I will...**

**add** _____

**remove** _____

**change** _____

**1.** My new design will work better because _____

_____

Day 3

**Name:** _____ **Date:** _____

**Directions:** Plan the tools and materials you will need. Plan your steps. Then, gather your materials, and rebuild your egg brain case.

## Tools and Materials

| Item Needed | Amount Needed | Item Needed | Amount Needed |
|---|---|---|---|
| | | | |
| | | | |
| | | | |

## Egg Brain Case Rebuilding Plan

| | Job, Task, or Role | Group Member(s) |
|---|---|---|
| 1 | | |
| 2 | | |
| 3 | | |
| 4 | | |
| 5 | | |
| 6 | | |
| 7 | | |
| 8 | | |

**Additional Notes**
(surprises, problems, solutions, etc.)

Name: _____ Date: _____

**Directions:** Repeat the steps to set up your test. Make adjustments as needed if you added new testing criteria. Test your redesigned egg brain case, and record the results. Then, answer the questions.

**Egg After Drop**

1. Describe the condition of the egg after the drop.

   _____

   _____

2. Describe the condition of the case after the drop.

   _____

   _____

3. Would you consider your new design successful? Explain your evidence.

   _____

   _____

   _____

4. Were your planned improvements successful? Explain your evidence.

   _____

   _____

**Name:** _____ **Date:** _____

**Directions:** Answer the questions to reflect on your egg brain case.

1. What are some ways your group worked well together?

_____

_____

_____

2. What about this challenge are you most proud of?

_____

_____

_____

3. What would you do differently next time if you had more time and materials?

_____

_____

_____

_____

4. What improvements would you make to the design of the human body for improved safety?

_____

_____

_____

_____

# Cells Teaching Support

## Overview of Unit Activities

Students will learn about and explore cells and cell parts through the following activities:

- reading about cells and cell theory
- reading about and studying pictures of cell organelles
- observing onion cells
- illustrating cell analogies
- interpreting a cell model diagram
- creating 3D animal cell models

## Materials Per Group

**Week 1**

- basic school supplies
- dropper
- iodine solution
- knife
- microscope
- microscope slide
- onion
- paper towels
- posterboard
- slide cover
- tweezers

**STEAM Challenge**

- basic school supplies
- building blocks/bricks
- cardboard pieces (various sizes)
- construction paper
- foam balls (2)
- modeling clay (different colors if possible)
- paper plate
- pipe cleaners (4–5)
- plastic wrap
- toothpicks (5–10)

## Setup and Instructional Tips

- **Safety Note:** Students need supervision when working with knives or other sharp instruments, such as in the Week 1 Day 3 (microscope) activity and if knives are needed for their cell model projects.

- **Week 1 Day 3:** If microscopes are not available, you may choose to display an onion cell image for students to observe.

- **STEAM Challenge:** The challenge can be done individually or in groups. Students working in groups should sketch their own designs first. Then, have them share designs in groups and choose one together.

## Discussion Questions

- If you could invent a new type of cell for your body, what function would it have?
- What are cells and what are they made of?
- How many cells do you think make up your body?
- What are the different types of cells?

## Additional Notes

- **Possible Misconception:** Cells and atoms are the same thing.
  **Truth:** Atoms are much smaller than cells. Cells are the smallest biological unit. Atoms are the smallest unit of a chemical element.

## Scaffolding and Extension Suggestions

- Support students as needed by giving them cell templates to build models on top of.
- Challenge students to build cell models with technology components, such as parts that light up or have programmable aspects.

## Answer Key

**Week 1 Day 1**
1. D
2. A
3. C

**Week 1 Day 2**
1. Both the cell membrane and the ticket-taker at a movie theater decide what or who gets inside.
2. brain; they both are in charge—the nucleus is the leader of the cell, and the brain is the leader of the body

**Week 1 Day 5**
1. plant, animal
2. nucleus
3. mitochondria (or mitochondrion)
4. cell membrane; controls what enters and leaves the cell
5. cell #1; it has a cell wall and a chloroplast

**Weeks 2 & 3**
See STEAM Challenge Rubric on page 221.

**Day 1**

Name: _____ Date: _____

**Directions:** Read the text, and choose the best answer for each question.

Cells are the basic unit of living things. Some living things are just one single cell. Most living things that you see, such as plants and animals, are made up of many cells working together. For example, you are made up of about a hundred trillion cells.

Since most cells are too small to be seen with the naked eye, cells were only discovered after the microscope was invented. It took time for people to realize that all living things were made up of cells. Then, people wondered where cells came from. Eventually they realized that cells came from…other cells! Cells divide to form new cells like themselves.

These ideas eventually were grouped together and called the *cell theory*. Three major ideas of cell theory are:

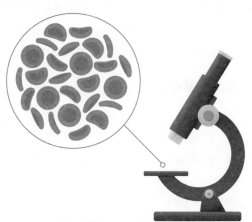

- All living things are made up of one or more cells.

- Cells are the basic unit of living things.

- All new cells come from cells that already exist.

**1.** If something is alive, it must be made of one or more _____.

   (A) water molecules

   (B) viruses

   (C) waves

   (D) cells

**2.** Which of these technologies was used to discover cells?

   (A) microscope

   (B) telescope

   (C) anemometer

   (D) thermometer

**3.** Which of these statements is NOT a main component of cell theory?

   (A) New cells come from existing cells.

   (B) Cells are the basic unit of life.

   (C) Cells can grow.

   (D) All living things are made up of one or more cells.

Day 2

**Name:** _____ **Date:** _____

**Directions:** Read the text, and study the diagrams. Then, answer the questions.

Cells have smaller parts inside them that work together to keep the cells alive. These cell parts are called organelles. Just as your organs (e.g., skin, brain, stomach) keep you alive, the organelles keep a cell alive.

The cell membrane surrounds a cell and allows things in or out. It keeps the right amount of stuff inside and prevents the wrong stuff from going in or out. Mitochondria turn oxygen and food into energy for a cell. A cell has a leader that tells the cell how to do its job. This leader is called the nucleus. The nucleus, mitochondria, and other organelles are all floating in a jelly-like liquid called the cytoplasm.

Plant cells have similar organelles to animal cells. Plants also have cell walls and chloroplasts. The cell wall is similar to the cell membrane, but it is stiffer and gives support to the plant. Plants can use sunlight to make energy. They do this in the chloroplast.

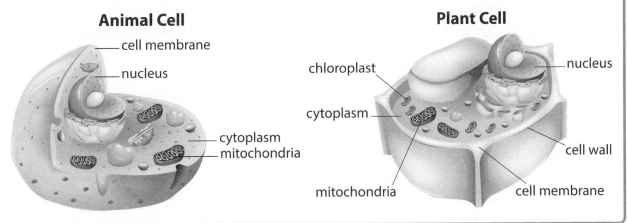

**Animal Cell**

cell membrane
nucleus
cytoplasm
mitochondria

**Plant Cell**

chloroplast
cytoplasm
nucleus
cell wall
mitochondria
cell membrane

1. In what way is the cell membrane similar to the person who collects tickets at the movie theater?

_____

_____

2. Which organ in the human body has a similar function to the nucleus in a cell? Explain your answer.

_____

_____

## Unit 6: Cells

Name: _____ Date: _____

**Directions:** Read through all the text once. Then, follow the steps to observe an onion cell.

> Onions are plants. Plants are living things. Cell theory tells us that onions must be made up of cells. Let's find the evidence!

### Materials

| | | | |
|---|---|---|---|
| dropper | iodine solution | knife | microscope |
| microscope slide and cover | onion | paper towels | tweezers |

### Steps

1. Cut the onion. Onions have layers. Pull out a small, single layer.

2. Use the tweezers to peel a thin layer of skin from the inside surface of your onion layer. (It should look like a piece of clear tape or plastic wrap.)

3. Lay the onion skin flat on the microscope slide.

4. Use the dropper to put one or two drops of iodine solution on the onion skin.

5. Wait a minute or two for the iodine to sink into the cells. (The purpose of the iodine is to stain the cell parts so you can see them more easily.)

6. Put a cover slip on top of the stained onion skin.

7. View the onion skin under the microscope using the 40x magnification on your microscope.

8. Draw what you see under the microscope. Label a cell membrane, a nucleus, and cytoplasm in your drawing.

**Day 4**

Name: _____  Date: _____

**Directions:** Making comparisons can help people understand how things work. Cells can be compared to things in the real world. For example, in the chart below a cell is compared to a factory. Study the chart. Then, complete the task.

| Cell Part | Cell Part Function | Factory Comparison | Similarities |
|---|---|---|---|
| cell membrane | controls what enters and leaves the cell | shipping and receiving department | controls what items enter and leave the factory |
| nucleus | in charge of what happens in the cell | factory boss | in charge of what happens in the factory |
| cytoplasm | contains all the cell parts (organelles) | factory floor | contains all the workers, machines, and other supplies |
| mitochondria | gives power to the cell | power plant | gives power (for example, electricity) to the factory |

**Task:** Create your own cell comparison. Some ideas include a castle, ranch, country, city, or movie theater. You can use one of those ideas or pick another. Fill in the chart. Then, draw a poster with your comparison, and label each of the four parts and explain how they are like the cell part. Use the factory example on this page as a guide.

| Cell Part | Cell Part Function | Comparison | Similarities |
|---|---|---|---|
| cell membrane | controls what enters and leaves the cell | | |
| nucleus | in charge of what happens in the cell | | |
| cytoplasm | contains all the cell parts (organelles) | | |
| mitochondria | gives power to the cell | | |

Day 5

Name: _____ Date: _____

**Directions:** Use the text and diagrams on page 105 to answer the questions.

### Cell 1

### Cell 2

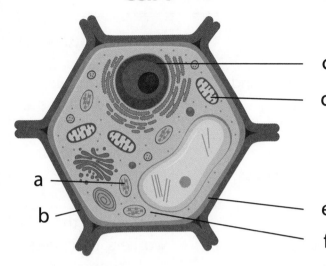
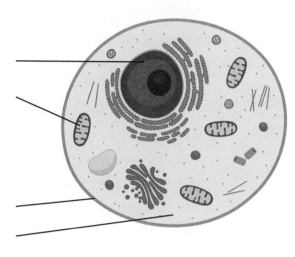

1. What two kinds of cells are shown here?

_____   _____

2. What is the name of organelle c? _____

3. What is the name of organelle d? _____

4. What is the name of organelle e, and what does it do?

_____

_____

5. Which of these cells is a plant cell?  How do you know?

_____

_____

**Day 1**

**Name:** _____ **Date:** _____

**Directions:** Read the text. Record the challenge criteria and constraints in the chart. Summarize the challenge in your own words. Then, write any questions you need answered before you begin the challenge.

# The Challenge

Scientists make models to better understand what they are studying. Sometimes those models tell them about relative sizes or other spatial relationships. Building models can also help you to remember something better.

Your challenge is to create a 3D model of an animal cell. You must label at least four parts: the nucleus, cell membrane, cytoplasm, and mitochondria. Including and labeling additional parts is optional. The names of the cell parts must be attached to the model. You must also include a description of each part's function. This may be attached or displayed however you choose. You may use the materials provided to you.

| Criteria for a Successful Cell Model | Constraints |
|---|---|
| | |
| | |
| | |

*Note: Your teacher may have additional constraints, such as time limits. You may add criteria if you choose to set additional goals.

## My Summary

_____

_____

## My Questions

_____

_____

Name: _____ Date: _____

**Directions:** Think about which materials would work best for your 3D model, and record your ideas in the chart. Then, brainstorm and record other notes or ideas for your design. Discuss ideas with others, and add to your brainstorming.

### Think About It!

What materials might you need, if any, to support a 3D model so it does not collapse?

What will you use for the cell part labels and how will you attach them to the model?

| Material | How It Might Help My Cell Model Design |
|----------|----------------------------------------|
|          |                                        |
|          |                                        |
|          |                                        |
|          |                                        |
|          |                                        |
|          |                                        |

**My Cell Model Brainstorming**

Name: _____ Date: _____

**Directions:** Sketch two or more designs for your cell model. Try to sketch some very different options. Label the parts and materials. Where appropriate, make note of the purpose for each part. Circle the design you think will work best. Or circle the ideas you will combine from multiple designs. Then, answer the question.

1. What concerns do you have about building your model?

_____

_____

## Unit 6: Cells

Name: _____ Date: _____

**Directions:** Plan the tools and materials you will need. Plan your steps. Then, gather your materials, and build your cell model. Record notes as you build.

### Tools and Materials

| Item Needed | Amount Needed | Item Needed | Amount Needed |
|---|---|---|---|
|  |  |  |  |
|  |  |  |  |
|  |  |  |  |

### Cell Model Building Plan

|  | Job, Task, or Role | Group Member(s) |
|---|---|---|
| 1 |  |  |
| 2 |  |  |
| 3 |  |  |
| 4 |  |  |
| 5 |  |  |
| 6 |  |  |
| 7 |  |  |
| 8 |  |  |

### Additional Notes
(problems, solutions, questions, etc.)

Name: _____ Date: _____

**Directions:** Present your 3D animal cell model to others. Ask them to evaluate your model and provide feedback. Evaluate and give feedback to other groups on their 3D animal cell models. For each group's model, draw a chart like the one below on a sheet of paper and write your comments. Remember these rules:

- Find at least two different ways to say something positive. What did you like about what they did in their model? Why was it good?

- Keep it friendly. Make sure your feedback is clear and constructive—that is, tell them how they could make it better.

| Criteria | Correctly Displayed on Cell ✓ | Correctly Lists Function ✓ | Comments |
|---|---|---|---|
| nucleus | | | |
| cell membrane | | | |
| cytoplasm | | | |
| mitochondria | | | |
| 3D component | | | |
| **Overall Neatness** | | | |
| **Overall Creativity** | | | |

## Talk About It!

Review your evaluations from other teams. Based on the feedback, how successful was your design? What did you learn from evaluating other teams' models?

## Unit 6: Cells

Name: _____ Date: _____

**Directions:** Reflect on your design, and answer the questions. Then, plan how you will improve it. Conduct additional research if needed.

1. What about your cell model worked well?

   _____

   _____

   _____

2. What changes do you want to make based on the feedback you received?

   _____

   _____

   _____

3. What different materials could you use in your model?

   _____

   _____

---

Draw a star next to one or more ways you will improve your design.

- My first design did not meet all the criteria because

  _____

  To improve it, I will _____

  _____

- Make parts of the model interactive or moveable.
- Make the model represent a specific type of animal cell (muscle, bone, etc.).
- Create a plant cell model to go with your animal cell.
- My own idea: _____

  _____

---

**Name:** _____ **Date:** _____

**Directions:** Plan your new cell model design. Then, sketch a few new designs. Label the parts and materials. Mark what is new or different, and circle the design you think will work best. Then, complete the sentence.

**In my redesign, I will…**

**add** _____

**remove** _____

**change** _____

1. My new design will serve as a better cell model because _____

_____

_____

**Unit 6: Cells**

**Name:** _____ **Date:** _____

**Directions:** Plan the tools and materials you will need. Plan your steps. Then, gather your materials, and rebuild your cell model.

### Tools and Materials

| Item Needed | Amount Needed | Item Needed | Amount Needed |
|---|---|---|---|
|  |  |  |  |
|  |  |  |  |
|  |  |  |  |

 **Quick Tip!**

You do not have to start from scratch! Make changes to your first cell model.

### Cell Model Rebuilding Plan

|  | Job, Task, or Role | Group Member(s) |
|---|---|---|
| 1 |  |  |
| 2 |  |  |
| 3 |  |  |
| 4 |  |  |
| 5 |  |  |
| 6 |  |  |
| 7 |  |  |
| 8 |  |  |

Name: _____ Date: _____

**Directions:** Present your new 3D cell model to others. Ask them to evaluate your model and provide feedback. Evaluate and give feedback to other groups on their 3D animal cell models. For each group's model, draw a chart like the one below on a sheet of paper and fill in your comments. Remember these rules:

- Find at least two different ways to say something positive. What did you like about what they did in their model? Why was it good?

- Keep it friendly. Make sure your feedback is clear and constructive—that is, tell them how they could make it better.

| Criteria | Correctly Displayed on Cell ✔ | Correctly Lists Function ✔ | Comments |
|---|---|---|---|
| nucleus | | | |
| cell membrane | | | |
| cytoplasm | | | |
| mitochondria | | | |
| 3D component | | | |
| **Overall Neatness** | | | |
| **Overall Creativity** | | | |

1. Based on the feedback, were you successful in improving your 3D cell model design? Explain your evidence.

_____

_____

Day 5

**Name:** _____ **Date:** _____

**Directions:** Answer the questions to reflect on your cell model.

1. What problems did you face and how did you handle them?

_____

_____

_____

2. What about this challenge are you most proud of?

_____

_____

3. What would you do differently next time if you had more time and materials?

_____

_____

_____

_____

4. What other types of models do you want to make?

_____

_____

# Plant Reproduction Teaching Support

## Overview of Unit Activities

Students will learn about and explore plant reproduction through the following activities:

- reading about DNA and sexual and asexual reproduction of plants
- reading about and studying pictures of the sexual reproduction of flowers
- matching flowers to their pollinators
- designing flowers for specific pollinators
- analyzing a line graph of plant growth data
- creating wind-powered seed dispersal vehicles

## Materials Per Group

**Week 1**

- basic school supplies

**STEAM Challenge**

- basic school supplies
- cardboard pieces
- coffee filters (3–4)
- construction paper
- fan
- foil
- grain of rice or large seed
- pipe cleaners (10–15)
- string (3–4 feet, 1 m)

## Setup and Instructional Tips

- **STEAM Challenge:** The challenge can be done individually or in groups. Students working in groups should sketch their own designs first. Then, have them share designs in groups and choose one together.

# Unit 7: Plant Reproduction

## Discussion Questions

- What is your favorite plant and why?
- How do plants affect your daily life?
- What do you think makes a weed different from any other plant?
- Why is seed dispersal important for plant reproduction?

## Additional Notes

- **Possible Misconception:** If offspring look more like one parent than the other, that means they inherited more DNA from that parent.
  **Truth:** Offspring created through sexual reproduction inherit the same amount of DNA from each parent.
- **Possible Design Solutions:** Students are likely to want to build helicopter style designs. Permit this, but remind students their design must be unique in some ways.

## Scaffolding and Extension Suggestions

- Support students as needed by having them first copy seed dispersal designs they find online. From there, they can make alterations.
- Challenge students to design vehicles that can be pushed by wind in water.

## Answer Key

**Week 1 Day 1**
1. B
2. C
3. A

**Week 1 Day 2**
1. Members of the population are unique. If there's a change in the environment that kills some members of the population, it may not kill all.
2. asexual reproduction because it only requires one parent
3. The pollen falls onto the stigma. A tube forms down the style and the pollen falls into the ovary where it fertilizes an egg in the ovule. The fertilized egg develops into a new seed.

**Week 1 Day 5**
1. 5 cm
2. 32 cm
3. 40 cm
4. Results do not show that music helped the plant to grow taller. In fact, it hindered growth.

**Weeks 2 & 3**
See STEAM Challenge Rubric on page 221.

Name: _____ Date: _____

**Directions:** Read the text, and choose the best answer for each question.

When living things reproduce, they pass on the instructions to make another member of that species. The instructions are called DNA. Only parents of the same species can make a child of that species. For example, oak tree parents can make more oak trees (by making an acorn). They cannot make a rose bush or a pine tree.

Many living things reproduce by combining parts from two parents. For example, a pumpkin reproduces by combining the pollen from a male pumpkin flower with the egg from a female pumpkin flower. This produces a pumpkin seed. In these cases, some DNA from the male parent and some from the female parent combine to form DNA for the child, or offspring. This is called sexual reproduction.

Many living things, including many plants, can reproduce asexually. Only one parent makes offspring. For example, the "eyes" of potatoes will sprout. Each of the sprouts can be cut from the potato and planted. They will each grow into a new potato plant. Since there is only one parent in asexual reproduction, there is no mixing of DNA. For this reason, offspring created asexually are clones of their parents. They have identical DNA.

**1.** Asexual reproduction requires _____.

  (A) 0 parents

  (B) 1 parent

  (C) 2 parents

  (D) 3 parents

**2.** The instructions for creating another member of the same species is called _____.

  (A) muscles

  (B) blood

  (C) DNA

**3.** Which of the following produces clones (exact copies) of the parent?

  (A) asexual reproduction

  (B) sexual reproduction

  (C) none of the above

  (D) both a and b

**Day 2**

Name: _____ Date: _____

**Directions:** Read the text, and study the diagram. Then, answer the questions.

One benefit of living things reproducing sexually is that their offspring are different from the parents and from each other. They all have different DNA. If a disease passes through, even if it kills many of the population, there is a chance that some members will have DNA with instructions to survive it. This means that at least some members of the species will survive to reproduce.

In sexual reproduction, an egg cell from a female joins with a sperm cell (pollen in plants) from a male. When they join, it is called *fertilization*. A fertilized cell eventually forms a new offspring—plant or animal. The offspring has half its DNA from the mother and half from the father, making a totally unique individual.

The flower shown in this image has male and female parts. They may fertilize themselves or fertilize other flowers. Imagine a bee visits the flower. Some of the pollen from the anther gets stuck on the bee. It flies to another flower. The pollen falls onto the stigma. A tube forms down the style, and the pollen falls into the ovary where it fertilizes an egg in the ovule. The fertilized egg develops into a new seed.

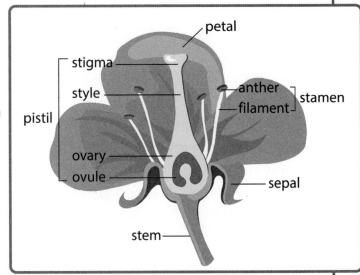

1. How can sexual reproduction benefit a species?

   _____

2. Which do you think might be a faster way to increase population size of a plant species quickly—sexual reproduction or asexual reproduction? Why?

   _____

   _____

3. Explain how pollen can get to the egg cells (ovules) in a flower.

   _____

   _____

**Name:** _____ **Date:** _____

**Directions:** Read the text, and complete the task.

Since flowers cannot travel to other flowers to mix their pollen and eggs, they rely on pollinators to carry their pollen for them. Some flowers are wind pollinated. They need the wind to blow their pollen to another plant of the same species. Others are pollinated by animals: bats, bees, birds, flies, etc. By looking at or smelling flowers, you can often get clues as to which kind of pollinator they use. For example:

- Flowers with beautiful scents and colors are often pollinated by bees.

- Flowers that smell like rotting meat are usually pollinated by flies.

- Flowers that do not look especially pretty but have large amounts of pollen that are easily blown off are generally pollinated by wind.

- Night-blooming, fruit-smelling flowers might have nocturnal bats as their pollinators.

- Flowers with beautiful colors, strong support, and nectar/pollen deep in the flower often are pollinated by birds, which perch on the flower and put long beaks deep inside the flower.

**Task:** Look at the photos and write what you think the pollinator is for each flower—wind, bats, bees, birds, or flies.

A _____

B _____

C _____

D _____

E _____

**Name:** _____ **Date:** _____

**Directions:** Read the text, and complete the task.

> Because plants depend on pollinators to take their pollen to another flower, they have evolved interesting strategies to make sure pollen gets to the right place. Some flowers are brightly colored and beautifully scented to attract bees, birds, and other pollinators. Others smell stinky to attract flies. Wind pollinated flowers do not bother being beautiful, but they have lots of pollen that is easily blown off the flower.

**Task:** Create an imaginary flower. Decide what you want its pollinator to be. Then, design the flower so that it maximizes the chances that its pollinator will take its pollen to the next flower. Draw and label your flower here.

© Shell Education

**Day 5**

Name: _____ Date: _____

**Directions:** Read the text, and study the graph. Then, answer the questions.

Plants may have the DNA instructions to grow tall, but if they do not get the nutrients they need, they may not reach their full potential height. Humans have experimented with ways to make plants grow taller or greener or produce bigger fruits or vegetables, etc. For her science fair project, Enola decided to see if growing bean seeds with classical music helped them grow faster. She graphed her results.

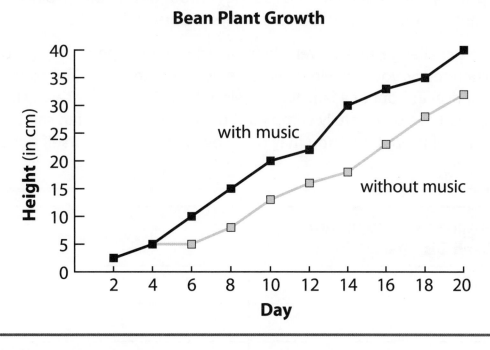

1. What did each plant measure on Day 4 of the experiment? _____

2. What did the plant grown without music measure on Day 20 of the experiment?

   _____

3. What did the plant grown with music measure on Day 20 of the experiment?

   _____

4. Based on these results, what can you conclude about the impact music has on bean plant growth?

   _____

   _____

## Unit 7: Plant Reproduction

Name: _____ Date: _____

**Directions:** Read the text. Record the challenge criteria and constraints in the chart. Summarize the challenge in your own words. Then, write any questions you need answered before you begin the challenge.

# The Challenge

If all seeds fell right below the parent plant and began growing there, they would compete with their parents for resources. For this reason, most plants disperse (spread) their seeds so they sprout farther away. Since most plants cannot move, they have special ways to spread their seeds around.

For this challenge, make a vehicle for a seed to be dispersed by wind (a fan). When ready, you will release your vehicle with the seed (for example, a grain of rice) in front of a fan. If it travels at least 10 feet (3 m) away from the fan, you have successfully completed the challenge. The fan can be the only source of propulsion. You may not blow on the seed yourself nor drag it with string.

| Criteria for a Successful Seed Dispersal Vehicle | Constraints |
|---|---|
|  |  |
|  |  |
|  |  |

\*Note: Your teacher may have additional constraints, such as time limits. You may add criteria if you choose to set additional goals.

## My Summary

_____

_____

## My Questions

_____

_____

_____

Name: _____ Date: _____

**Directions:** Conduct additional research about how different seeds travel via wind. Draw and describe two examples from your findings. Then, brainstorm and record other notes or ideas for your design. Discuss ideas with others, and add to your brainstorming.

| Example 1 | Example 2 |
|---|---|
|  |  |

**My Seed Dispersal Vehicle Brainstorming**

 **Think About It!**

Will your seed go inside the vehicle, or will the vehicle somehow attach to the seed?

**Day 3**

Name: _____ Date: _____

**Directions:** Sketch two or more designs for your seed dispersal vehicle. Label the parts and materials. Where appropriate, make note of the purpose for each part. Circle the design you think will work best. Or circle the ideas you will combine from multiple designs. Then, answer the question.

**1.** What concerns do you have about your design?

_____

_____

**Name:** _____ **Date:** _____

**Directions:** Plan the tools and materials you will need. Plan your steps. Then, gather your materials, and build your seed dispersal vehicle. Record notes as you build.

### Tools and Materials

| Item Needed | Amount Needed | Item Needed | Amount Needed |
|---|---|---|---|
|  |  |  |  |
|  |  |  |  |
|  |  |  |  |

### Seed Dispersal Vehicle Building Plan

|  | Job, Task, or Role | Group Member(s) |
|---|---|---|
| 1 |  |  |
| 2 |  |  |
| 3 |  |  |
| 4 |  |  |
| 5 |  |  |
| 6 |  |  |
| 7 |  |  |
| 8 |  |  |

### Additional Notes
(surprises, problems, solutions, etc.)

**Day 5**

Name: _____ Date: _____

**Directions:** Follow the directions to set up your test. Test your seed dispersal vehicle and record the results. Then, answer the questions.

1. Adjust the fan to approximately waist-level height. Keep the fan height the same for each test.

2. Hold the vehicle with the seed about 5 inches (13 cm) in front of the fan and release it.

3. Measure and record how far the vehicle traveled from the fan.

4. Repeat the test five times and record the results.

5. Use your longest distance to determine if your design was successful.

| Trial | Distance Traveled (note units) |
|:---:|:---|
| 1 | |
| 2 | |
| 3 | |
| 4 | |
| 5 | |

1. Based on these results, was your seed dispersal vehicle successful?

_____

_____

2. What did you notice about other designs that were successful?

_____

_____

_____

Name: _____ Date: _____

**Directions:** Reflect on your design, and answer the questions. Then, plan how you will improve it. Conduct additional research if needed.

1. What about your seed dispersal vehicle worked well?

   _____

   _____

   _____

2. What flaws did you discover in your design?

   _____

   _____

   _____

Draw a star next to one or more ways you will improve your design.

- My first design did not meet all the criteria because

   _____

   To improve it, I will _____

   _____

- Design the vehicle to move 50 percent farther than it did the first time.

- Design the vehicle to carry five seeds at a time.

- My own idea: _____

   _____

**Day 2**

**Name:** _____ **Date:** _____

**Directions:** Plan your new seed dispersal vehicle design. Then, sketch a few new designs. Label the parts and materials. Mark what is new or different, and circle the design you think will work best. Then, complete the sentence.

**In my redesign, I will...**

**add** _____

**remove** _____

**change** _____

**1.** My new design will work better because _____

_____

_____

**Name:** _____ **Date:** _____

**Directions:** Plan the tools and materials you will need. Plan your steps. Then, gather your materials, and rebuild your seed dispersal vehicle.

## Tools and Materials

| Item Needed | Amount Needed | Item Needed | Amount Needed |
|---|---|---|---|
|  |  |  |  |
|  |  |  |  |
|  |  |  |  |

## Seed Dispersal Vehicle Rebuilding Plan

|  | Job, Task, or Role | Group Member(s) |
|---|---|---|
| 1 |  |  |
| 2 |  |  |
| 3 |  |  |
| 4 |  |  |
| 5 |  |  |
| 6 |  |  |
| 7 |  |  |
| 8 |  |  |

### Additional Notes
(surprises, problems, solutions, etc.)

**Day 4**

Name: _____ Date: _____

**Directions:** Follow the directions to set up your test. Test your seed dispersal vehicle, and record the results. Then, answer the questions.

| Trial | Distance Traveled (note units) |
|-------|-------------------------------|
| 1 | |
| 2 | |
| 3 | |
| 4 | |
| 5 | |

1. In what ways was your redesign better than your original design?

_____

_____

_____

2. Were there ways that your redesign wasn't as good as the original? If so, explain how.

_____

_____

_____

**Name:** _____  **Date:** _____

**Directions:** Reflect on your experience building and improving your seed dispersal vehicle by filling in the chart.

Something I Would
Like to Improve

My Favorite Thing
about the Design

**Image of Our
Best Design**

Something I Learned

Something That
Was Difficult

# Air and Weather Teaching Support

## Overview of Unit Activities

Students will learn about and explore air masses and weather through the following activities:

- reading about air masses
- reading about and studying pictures of warm and cold fronts
- building anemometers and measuring wind speed
- creating tornadoes in bottles
- analyzing a bar graph of tornado data
- creating parachutes for small, lightweight items

## Materials Per Group

**Week 1**

- basic school supplies
- duct tape
- empty 2L bottles (2; no lids)
- fan
- food coloring
- glitter
- paper cups (4)
- paper plate
- permanent marker
- stopwatch
- thumbtack with plastic end
- washer
- water

**STEAM Challenge**

- basic school supplies
- characters to drop (2 that are identical; toy dolls, stuffed animals, etc.)
- construction paper
- napkins (4–5)
- newspaper
- paper towel roll
- plastic bag
- plastic wrap
- string (4–5 feet, 1.5 m)
- thread (4–5 feet, 1.5 m)
- tissue paper
- washers

## Setup and Instructional Tips

- **Safety Note:** Make sure that no one is below during testing and that students are supervised when standing at tall heights. Ladders can be dangerous. Consider a low (one-story) balcony for testing the parachutes.
- **STEAM Challenge:** The challenge can be done individually or in groups. Students working in groups should sketch their own designs first. Then, have them share designs in groups and choose one together.

## Discussion Questions

- Have you ever experienced extreme weather, such as thunderstorms, hurricanes, tornadoes, etc.? What was the experience like?
- What happens when warm and cold air interact?
- What are some ways to prepare for extreme weather events?
- How good of a job do you think meteorologists do at predicting the weather? What about the job would be difficult?
- What is your favorite kind of weather—sunny, snowy, rainy, or something else? Why?

## Additional Notes

- **Possible Misconception:** Lightning never strikes the same place twice.
  **Truth:** Lightning often strikes the highest point in a given area and so is likely to strike those places multiple times. Skyscrapers, for example, have been struck many times.

## Scaffolding and Extension Suggestions

- Support students as needed by having them create parachutes for smaller items.
- Challenge students to drop their parachutes in windy conditions, either on a windy day, or by adding fans to the testing area.

## Answer Key

**Week 1 Day 1**
1. A
2. B
4. A

**Week 1 Day 2**
1. weather
2. Answer should describe the local weather.
3. Answer should describe the climate or local region.
4. rain or snow

**Week 1 Day 5**
1. Texas
2. Answers may vary but generally southeast and Midwest/central.

**Weeks 2 & 3**
See STEAM Challenge Rubric on page 221.

Name: _____ Date: _____

**Directions:** Read the text, and choose the best answer for each question.

Most of the air on Earth (78 percent) is nitrogen. About 21 percent is oxygen. There are also small amounts of other gases, such as carbon dioxide.

Air moves around Earth. Sometimes there is a large amount of air that stays in one place at a time. That is called an air mass. All the air in an air mass has a similar temperature and amount of water vapor in it. The kind of weather you are having today is probably caused by the type of air mass in your area.

Air masses are named for where they formed. They have two names: the first one tells you about the humidity. For example, maritime air masses form over water and likely have higher humidity. Continental air masses form over land and probably have lower humidity. The second name tells you about the temperature. Tropical air masses formed in warm areas and are probably warm. Polar air masses are colder. These are some examples of air masses:

- Continental Polar
- Continental Tropical
- Maritime Tropical
- Maritime Polar

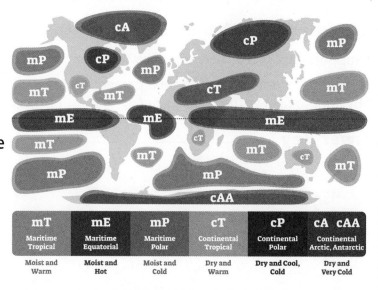

| mT | mE | mP | cT | cP | cA cAA |
|---|---|---|---|---|---|
| Maritime Tropical | Maritime Equatorial | Maritime Polar | Continental Tropical | Continental Polar | Continental Arctic, Antarctic |
| Moist and Warm | Moist and Hot | Moist and Cold | Dry and Warm | Dry and Cool, Cold | Dry and Very Cold |

**1.** The air we breathe is mostly made of __.

   (A) nitrogen          (C) water vapor

   (B) oxygen           (D) carbon dioxide

**2.** An air mass _____.

   (A) has very different temperatures and amounts of water vapor through it

   (B) has very similar temperatures and amounts of water vapor through it

**3.** What type of air mass formed over land near one of the poles?

   (A) Continental Polar        (C) Maritime Tropical

   (B) Continental Tropical      (D) Maritime Polar

**Name:** _____ **Date:** _____

**Directions:** Read the text, and study the diagrams. Then, answer the questions.

Weather is what the atmosphere is like at a certain time and place. Weather includes things such as temperature, air speed and direction, how sunny or snowy or rainy it is, over several days. Climate tells you what the average weather is like in an area over many years.

Weather is caused by air masses over your area. Wind and air currents cause air masses to move, usually causing the weather to change. Thunderstorms may happen at the edge of air masses.

cold front

A front is the border between two air masses. There are cold fronts and warm fronts. As the name tells you, cold fronts bring colder air into the area. A warm front brings warm air into an area. The arrival of either front causes warm air to rise, which often brings rain or snow. Cold fronts tend to bring heavier rain or snow than warm fronts. When two air masses meet but stay more or less in the same place, this is called a stationary front.

warm front

1. Is the following a description of weather or climate?

   *"Today's temperatures are a high of 81° and a low of 64° with 4 mile/hour winds out of the northwest and a 10% chance of rain."*

   _____

2. What is the weather today in your neighborhood?

   _____

3. Describe the climate in the area where you live. (It is okay to look up this information online.)

   _____

4. When a new front arrives, what often comes with it? _____

**Day 3**

Name: _____ Date: _____

**Directions:** Wind speed is part of a weather report. It is measured with a tool called an anemometer. Read all the text through once. Then, follow the steps to build and use an anemometer.

---

**Materials**

| | | | |
|---|---|---|---|
| fan | four paper cups | paper plate | pencil with an eraser |
| permanent marker | stopwatch | tape | thumbtack with plastic end |

---

**Steps**

1. Clearly mark the outside of one cup with the permanent marker. You can draw anything you like on it, so it looks different from the others.

2. Use tape to attach one cup to the edge of the plate. The cup should be on its side with the opening facing left. Turn the plate and attach the rest of the cups the same way.

3. Punch the thumbtack through the middle of the plate. Pin the plate to the eraser on the pencil.

4. Hold up the plate and blow on it to make sure the cups spin. If not, readjust until they do.

5. Take the plate outside on a windy day (or do this inside near a fan). Keep track of how many times the marked cup goes around per 30 seconds. This is the wind speed.

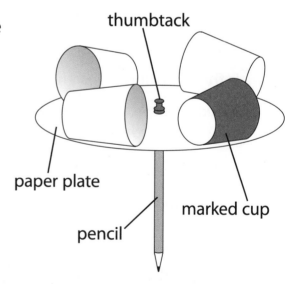

**Try This!**

Make a chart and record the wind speed in your area over several days. Compare it to the wind speed given in your local weather report. Notice the units for wind speed in your local weather report.

Name: _____ Date: _____

**Directions:** Tornadoes are dangerous. But if you are not anywhere near one, it is exciting to look at the spinning vortex of air. Follow the steps to create a tornado in a bottle!

| **Materials** | | |
| --- | --- | --- |
| duct tape | food coloring | glitter |
| two empty 2L bottles (no lids) | washer | water |

**Steps**

1. Fill one bottle with water.

2. Lay the washer on top.

3. Put the empty bottle on top of the washer.

4. Wrap duct tape around the two bottle necks so they are securely attached.

5. Make your tornado: Turn the contraption upside down so the water is in the top bottle. Make quick circular motions to get the water spinning. Watch the tornado appear in the water!

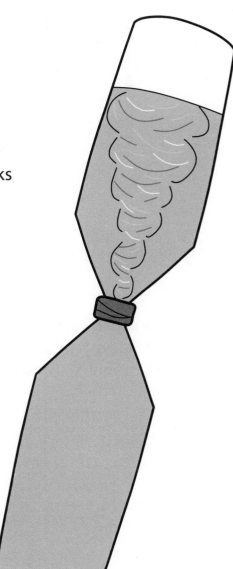

**Day 5**

Name: _____ Date: _____

**Directions:** The graph shows the U.S. states that get the most tornadoes per year. It tells you, on average, how many they have. Study the graph. Then, answer the questions.

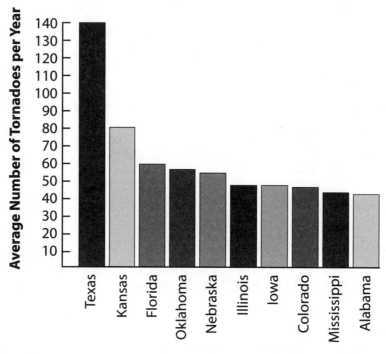

**10 U.S. States with the Most Tornadoes**

1. According to this graph, which U.S. state gets the most tornadoes per year?

   _____

2. On the map, shade in the 10 states listed on the graph. What region(s) of the United States get the most tornadoes—northeast, southeast, northwest, southwest, central/Midwest? (More than one answer is acceptable.)

   _____

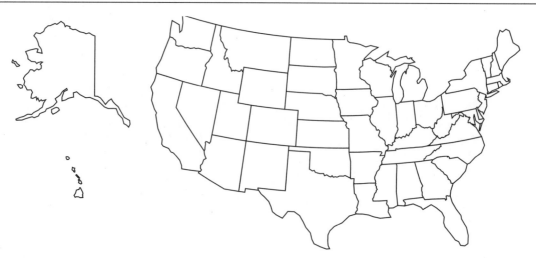

Name: _____ Date: _____

**Directions:** Read the text. Record the challenge criteria and constraints in the chart. Summarize the challenge in your own words. Then, write any questions you need answered before you begin the challenge.

## The Challenge

Understanding weather requires an understanding of air. Once you know about air, this knowledge can help with all sorts of things, including engineering useful items such as parachutes. Parachutes are a very interesting use of air resistance. *Air resistance* is a force that is caused by air. When a parachute drops, gravity pulls it down. Air resistance works against gravity. Air resistance slows the parachute down.

Your challenge is to create a parachute. You will attach it to a small, lightweight toy. You will have a second identical toy with no parachute. When dropped from a one-story height at the same time, your toy with the parachute attached must fall to the ground more slowly than the one without a parachute. You may use the supplies provided to you. You may decide if you wish the parachute to unfold or if you want to drop it while already in the open position.

| Criteria for a Successful Parachute | Constraints |
|---|---|
|  |  |
|  |  |
|  |  |

*Note: Your teacher may have additional constraints, such as time limits. You may add criteria if you choose to set additional goals.

### My Summary

_____

_____

### My Questions

_____

_____

Day 2

Name: _____  Date: _____

**Directions:** Conduct research about parachute designs as needed. Answer the questions based on your findings. Think about which materials would work best, and record your ideas in the chart. Then, brainstorm and record other notes or ideas for your design. Discuss ideas with others, and add to your brainstorming.

**1.** How do parachutes work?

_____

_____

**2.** What is similar about most parachute designs?

_____

_____

**3.** What materials are used in real parachutes?

_____

| Material | How It Might Help My Parachute Design |
|---|---|
|  |  |
|  |  |
|  |  |
|  |  |
|  |  |

**My Parachute Brainstorming**

**Name:** _____ **Date:** _____

**Directions:** Sketch two or more designs for your parachute. Label the parts and materials. Where appropriate, make note of the purpose for each part. Circle the design you think will work best. Or circle the ideas you will combine from multiple designs. Then, answer the question.

**1.** What concerns do you have about your design?

_____

_____

## Unit 8: Air and Weather

Name: _____  Date: _____

**Directions:** Plan the tools and materials you will need. Plan your steps. Then, gather your materials, and build your parachute. Record notes as you build.

### Tools and Materials

| Item Needed | Amount Needed | Item Needed | Amount Needed |
|---|---|---|---|
|  |  |  |  |
|  |  |  |  |
|  |  |  |  |

### Parachute Building Plan

|  | Job, Task, or Role | Group Member(s) |
|---|---|---|
| 1 |  |  |
| 2 |  |  |
| 3 |  |  |
| 4 |  |  |
| 5 |  |  |
| 6 |  |  |
| 7 |  |  |
| 8 |  |  |

### Additional Notes
(surprises, problems, solutions, etc.)

Name: _____ Date: _____

**Directions:** Follow the directions to set up and perform your test. Record the results. Then, answer the questions.

1. Attach one toy to your parachute. Leave the other toy without a parachute.

2. Drop both from the same height (one story) at the same time.

3. Time how long it takes the parachute character to reach the ground.

4. Repeat the drop test five times.

| Trial | Time It Took Parachute Toy to Fall to the Ground (seconds) | Slower than Toy with No Parachute? (yes/no) |
|-------|-----------------------------------------------------------|---------------------------------------------|
| 1 | | |
| 2 | | |
| 3 | | |
| 4 | | |
| 5 | | |

1. What other observation did you make about how your parachute performed?

_____

_____

2. Was your parachute successful? What is your evidence?

_____

_____

Name: _____ Date: _____

**Directions:** Reflect on your design, and answer the questions. Then, plan how you will improve it. Conduct additional research if needed.

**1.** What about your parachute worked well?

_____

_____

_____

**2.** What aspects did not work well or could be improved?

_____

_____

_____

Draw a star next to one or more ways you will improve your design.

- My first design did not meet all the criteria because

_____

To improve it, I will _____

_____

- Reduce the speed of the falling parachute. It will take at least _____ seconds longer to hit the ground.

- Add designs to your parachute so it can be easily recognized as yours.

- My own idea: _____

_____

**Name:** _____ **Date:** _____

**Directions:** Plan your new parachute design. Then, sketch a few new designs. Label the parts and materials. Mark what is new or different, and circle the design you think will work best. Then, complete the sentence.

**In my redesign, I will…**

**add** _____

**remove** _____

**change** _____

**1.** My new design will work better because _____

_____

_____

Name: _____ Date: _____

**Directions:** Plan the tools and materials you will need. Plan your steps. Then, gather your materials, and rebuild your parachute.

## Tools and Materials

| Item Needed | Amount Needed | Item Needed | Amount Needed |
|---|---|---|---|
|  |  |  |  |
|  |  |  |  |
|  |  |  |  |

## Parachute Rebuilding Plan

|  | Job, Task, or Role | Group Member(s) |
|---|---|---|
| 1 |  |  |
| 2 |  |  |
| 3 |  |  |
| 4 |  |  |
| 5 |  |  |
| 6 |  |  |
| 7 |  |  |
| 8 |  |  |

### Additional Notes
(surprises, problems, solutions, etc.)

Name: _____ Date: _____

**Directions:** Repeat the steps to set up your test. Test your redesigned parachute, and record the results. Then, answer the questions.

| Trial | Time It Took Parachute Toy to Fall to the Ground (seconds) | Slower than Toy with No Parachute? (yes/no) |
|---|---|---|
| 1 | | |
| 2 | | |
| 3 | | |
| 4 | | |
| 5 | | |

1. Was your new design successful in meeting all your goals? Explain your evidence.

   _____

   _____

   _____

2. Which parachute design performed better? Explain your evidence.

   _____

   _____

   _____

## Unit 8: Air and Weather

**Name:** _____ **Date:** _____

**Directions:** Answer the questions to reflect on your parachute.

1. What about this challenge was difficult?

   _____

   _____

   _____

2. What about this challenge are you most proud of?

   _____

   _____

   _____

3. What advice would you give to someone who wants to make their own parachute?

   _____

   _____

   _____

4. Would you jump out of a plane with a parachute? Why or why not?

   _____

   _____

   _____

# Earth's Materials Teaching Support

## Overview of Unit Activities

Students will learn about and explore Earth's layers and materials through the following activities:

- reading about Earth's layers
- reading about and studying pictures of rock cycles
- labeling parts of the rock cycle
- creating model rocks with crayons
- identify crystals from their shapes and hardness
- designing procedures to grow sugar crystals

## Materials Per Group

### Week 1

- basic school supplies
- crayons (multiple colors)
- potholder
- peeler, pencil sharpener, and/or plastic knife

### STEAM Challenge

- basic school supplies
- craft sticks (2)
- edible sprinkles (optional)
- flavoring (optional; such as peppermint, lemon, or cinnamon)
- foil
- food coloring
- glass jars or similar heat-resistant containers (2; for growing crystals)
- heat-resistant, food-grade container (for dissolving sugar)
- potholder
- string (2–3 feet, 1 m)
- sugar (4 cups, 800 g)
- water
- wooden skewers (2)

## Setup and Instructional Tips

- **Safety Notes:** Adult supervision is needed for the peeler and hot water during the crayon activity on Week 1 Day 4. Use potholders and spoons to avoid getting burned.

- Adult supervision is needed when boiling water, dissolving sugar, and pouring the hot liquid for the STEAM challenge. If this is not possible, consider having students make salt crystals instead. No boiling is required, but the result is not edible.

- **Timing:** Once students have set up their crystal growing stations, it is ideal to allow at least three weeks for crystals to form. To speed up the process, place growing stations in cool, dry locations. You can place them in a refrigerator, but crystal formations will be smaller.

### Discussion Questions

- What makes up Earth?
- Did you ever find and keep a specific rock? Why do you think people do this?
- Would you want to explore in deep caves or study volcanoes? Why or why not?

### Additional Notes

- **Possible Misconception:** Earth's mantle is a liquid.
  **Truth:** The mantle is a solid but one that flows a bit like a liquid.
- **Possible Design Solutions:** Students may try different solutions of sugar and water. The best will be those that are highly saturated with sugar. Rolling the strings or sticks in some sugar is also a good strategy to give the crystals starting points.

### Scaffolding and Extension Suggestions

- Support students with growing crystals by allowing them to start with actual rock candy and see if they can make it grow bigger.
- Challenge students to grow crystals into unique shapes.

### Answer Key

**Week 1 Day 1**
1. A
2. C

3. C

**Week 1 Day 2**
1. small crystals because lava usually cools quickly on the surface or in the ocean
2. It is called a cycle because each rock can change into other types of rock. This can happen again and again in a circle, or cycle.

**Week 1 Day 3**

### Rock Cycle

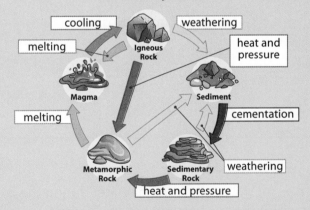

**Week 1 Day 5**
1. talc
2. A and B

3. talc, gypsum, calcite, and fluorite
4. 4

**Weeks 2 & 3**
See STEAM Challenge Rubric on page 221.

**Day 1**

Name: _____ Date: _____

**Directions:** Read the text, and choose the best answer for each question.

We walk on the surface of Earth. This surface—called the crust—includes the land beneath our feet, the oceans, and the land beneath the oceans. The land beneath our feet is called the *continental crust*, and the land beneath the oceans is the *oceanic crust*. The thickness of the crust varies. Under the ocean it might only be 5 km (3 miles), under your feet it might be 30 km (18 miles), and at the top of a mountain it could be 100 km (62 miles). The average thickness is about 17 km (10.5 miles). Even though the crust is the thinnest layer, no one has ever been able to dig a hole through it.

The layer below the crust is the mantle. Even though it is a solid, it is under so much heat and pressure that it can flow slowly like a liquid! We see bits of the mantle when some of it rises out of Earth during volcanic eruptions.

At the center of Earth is an iron core. The outer core is liquid, and the inner core is solid.

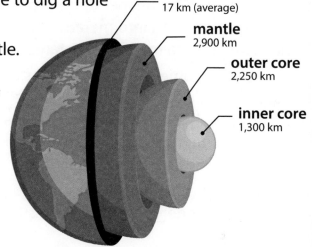

crust
17 km (average)

mantle
2,900 km

outer core
2,250 km

inner core
1,300 km

1. Which of Earth's four layers is the thinnest?

　Ⓐ crust

　Ⓑ mantle

　Ⓒ outer core

　Ⓓ inner core

2. Which natural event sometimes brings a bit of the mantle to Earth's surface?

　Ⓐ hurricanes

　Ⓑ tornadoes

　Ⓒ volcanoes

　Ⓓ tsunamis

3. Earth's magnetic field comes from flowing iron currents. Which one of Earth's layers do you think most likely makes up Earth's magnetic field?

　Ⓐ crust

　Ⓑ mantle

　Ⓒ outer core

　Ⓓ inner core

**Name:** _____  **Date:** _____

**Directions:** Read the text, and study the pictures. Then, answer the questions.

Earth and its materials are always changing. The process of rocks changing is called *the rock cycle*.

Wind and water can cause rocks to break down into smaller pieces. This process is called *weathering*. The small pieces may be sediments, soil, and sand. Sometimes those small pieces layer on top of each other and harden into new rocks. That process is called *cementation*. The new rocks that form from those pieces are sedimentary rocks.

Some rocks are deeper underground. With enough pressure and heat over time, they may turn into metamorphic rocks. Limestone is a sedimentary rock that can turn into marble (a metamorphic rock) with a lot of heat and pressure.

Lava that comes out of volcanoes eventually cools and hardens into rocks. Those are called igneous rocks. Some igneous rocks have crystals in them. Larger crystals usually form in rocks that cooled slowly—often from magma that cooled underground. Lava that comes to the surface or erupts in the ocean tends to cool very quickly.

Igneous rocks can break down into pieces and form sedimentary rocks. Or they can undergo heat and pressure and turn into metamorphic rocks.

| sedimentary rock | metamorphic rock | igneous rock |

1. What size crystals would you expect in lava that cooled into igneous rocks on Earth's surface or in the ocean? Explain your reasoning.

_____

_____

2. Why is the process of rocks changing considered a cycle?

_____

_____

**Name:** _____ **Date:** _____

**Directions:** Use the terms provided to label the rock cycle action happening at each arrow to cause the changes between rocks. Terms may be used more than once. Hint: Arrows with the same shade have the same label.

| cooling | cementation | heat and pressure | melting | weathering |

# Rock Cycle

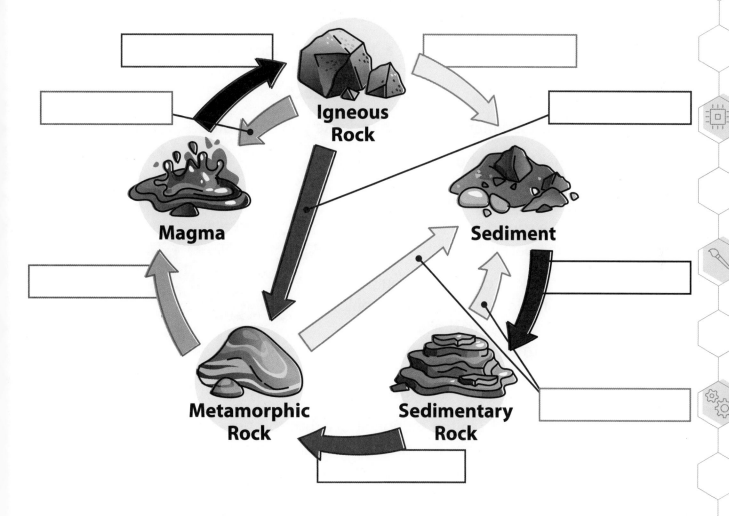

## Unit 9: Earth's Materials

Name: _____ Date: _____

**Directions:** Use crayons to model the formation of igneous, sedimentary, and metamorphic rocks. Follow the steps for each rock type. Create labels for each rock, and put them on display.

### Sedimentary Rock

1. Create "sediment" by scraping off bits of several different colors of crayon with a peeler, pencil sharpener, and/or plastic knife.

2. Once you have a small pile of sediment, wrap it in aluminum foil and stand on it to represent the rock being layered and cemented into a new rock.

3. Unwrap it, and you should have a new sedimentary crayon rock.

### Metamorphic Rock

1. Form another sedimentary crayon rock like you did in step 1 above.

2. Make a small boat out of the aluminum foil, and float your boat in hot water. Watch as the crayon melts a little into layers. Use a spoon with a potholder to remove the boat.

3. Allow your rock to cool. You should see layers of color in your metamorphic crayon rock. These are similar to the layers that form in metamorphic rock.

### Igneous Rock

1. Repeat steps 1 and 2 in the section above, but this time leave the boat floating until the crayons completely melt into liquid, the colors mix, and you no longer see separate pieces or layers.

2. Use a spoon with a potholder to remove the boat from the water and allow the rock to cool. This represents an igneous rock.

igneous      sedimentary      metamorphic

**Name:** _____ **Date:** _____

**Directions:** Read the text, and study the chart. Then, answer the questions.

Rocks are made of minerals. Some minerals are very soft. You can scratch them with your fingernails. Others are hard. Almost no other mineral will scratch them. A geologist named Mohs used 10 minerals to create a hardness scale to help identify minerals. The softest mineral on his scale is talc. It is a 1, and that means that anything harder than a 1 can scratch talc. Diamond is a 10, which means it is the hardest. Diamonds can scratch all the other minerals in the chart, and none of them can scratch diamonds.

**Mohs Scale of Mineral Hardness**

| 1 | 2 | 3 | 4 | 5 |
|---|---|---|---|---|
|  |  |  |  |  |
| Talc | Gypsum | Calcite | Fluorite | Apatite |

| 6 | 7 | 8 | 9 | 10 |
|---|---|---|---|---|
|  |  | | | |
| Orthoclase | Quartz | Topaz | Corundum | Diamond |

1. Which mineral listed on Mohs scale can be scratched by gypsum?

   _____

2. Which of these minerals can topaz scratch? (Select all correct answers.)
   - (A) Orthoclase
   - (B) Fluorite
   - (C) Corundum
   - (D) Diamond

3. Magnetite is a naturally magnetic mineral. It is not shown in Mohs hardness scale. It has a hardness between 5 and 6. Which four minerals shown on Mohs hardness scale could magnetite scratch?

   _____    _____

   _____    _____

4. You found a mineral that can scratch calcite. A piece of apatite put a scratch in your mineral sample. What would you guess is the hardness of your mystery mineral?

   _____

Name: _____ Date: _____

**Directions:** Read the text. Record the challenge criteria and constraints in the chart. Summarize the challenge in your own words. Then, write any questions you need answered before you begin the challenge.

## The Challenge

If you look closely at sugar or salt under a microscope, you will see they have a crystalline structure. When heated and then allowed to cool slowly, the crystals will cling together to form larger crystals. This is how a sweet treat called rock candy is made. It also mirrors the process of crystal formation in nature because larger crystals tend to grow when given time to cool slowly.

Your challenge is to design a procedure to make a homemade sugar crystal (or mass of crystals) that could be eaten as a candy. You may use sugar and water (as well as food coloring and flavorings). You may use a maximum of 4 cups (800 g) of sugar. You decide how much water. You may choose the container (it needs to be heat proof!). You may also select the surface on which your crystals will grow—such as a string or a stick—and how it will be set up to grow. You have three weeks to grow your crystal. You may use materials provided to you.

| Criteria for a Successful Sugar Crystal Procedure | Constraints |
|---|---|
| | |
| | |
| | |

*Note: Your teacher may have additional constraints, such as time limits. You may add criteria if you choose to set additional goals.

### My Summary

_____

_____

### My Questions

_____

_____

Name: _____ Date: _____

**Directions:** Conduct research about how others have successfully grown sugar crystals. Draw some examples of crystal growing setups. Record any other tips you learn. Then, brainstorm and record other notes or ideas for your crystal growing procedure. Discuss ideas with others, and add to your brainstorming.

| **Example 1** | **Example 2** |
|---|---|
| | |
| **Example 3** | **Example 4** |
| | |

**My Sugar Crystal Brainstorming**

Name: _____ Date: _____

**Directions:** Sketch two or more designs for your crystal growing setup. Label the parts and materials. Circle the design you think will work best. Or circle the ideas you will combine from multiple designs. Then, record the steps to make your solution and grow your crystals.

**Sugar Crystal Procedure**

### Think About It!

How will your crystal growing procedure be unique?

Name: _____ Date: _____

**Directions:** Plan the tools and materials you will need. Plan your steps. Then, gather your materials. Follow your procedure to make your solution. Record notes as you build. Place your setup in a cool, dry location.

## Tools and Materials

| Item Needed | Amount Needed | Item Needed | Amount Needed |
|---|---|---|---|
|  |  |  |  |
|  |  |  |  |
|  |  |  |  |

## Sugar Crystal Building Plan

|  | Job, Task, or Role | Group Member(s) |
|---|---|---|
| 1 |  |  |
| 2 |  |  |
| 3 |  |  |
| 4 |  |  |
| 5 |  |  |
| 6 |  |  |
| 7 |  |  |
| 8 |  |  |

## Additional Notes
(surprises, problems, solutions, etc.)

**Name:** _____ **Date:** _____

**Directions:** After three weeks (or other determined time) of observing your crystal grow, remove it from the solution and setup you created. Measure it and record the results. Then, answer the questions.

**Length of Crystal at the Longest Point:** _____

### Photo or Sketch of Your Crystal

1. How long was your crystal growing? _____

2. What did you notice about the crystal as it changed and grew (or did not grow) before the final day?

   _____

   _____

3. Was your procedure to grow a sugar crystal successful? What is your evidence?

   _____

   _____

   _____

Name: _____  Date: _____

**Directions:** Reflect on your design, and answer the questions. Then, plan how you will improve it. Conduct additional research if needed.

**1.** What about your sugar crystal procedure worked well?

_____

_____

_____

**2.** What did you notice about the procedures and setups of groups that were able to grow large crystals?

_____

_____

_____

Draw a star next to one or more ways you will improve your design.

- My first design did not meet all the criteria because

  _____

  To improve it, I will _____

  _____

- Make it grow twice as big.

- Improve the visual appeal and flavor of the rock candy.

- My own idea: _____

  _____

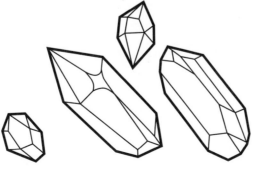

**Name:** _____ **Date:** _____

**Directions:** Plan your new crystal growing procedure. Then, sketch a few new setup designs. Circle the design you think will work best. Record the new steps to make your solution.

**In my redesign, I will…**

**add** _____

**remove** _____

**change** _____

**New Sugar Crystal Procedure**

**Name:** _____ **Date:** _____

**Directions:** Plan the tools and materials you will need. Plan your steps. Then, gather your materials. Follow your new procedure to make your solution. Record notes as you build. Place your set up in a cool, dry location.

### Tools and Materials

| Item Needed | Amount Needed | Item Needed | Amount Needed |
|---|---|---|---|
|  |  |  |  |
|  |  |  |  |
|  |  |  |  |

### Sugar Crystal Rebuilding Plan

|  | Job, Task, or Role | Group Member(s) |
|---|---|---|
| 1 |  |  |
| 2 |  |  |
| 3 |  |  |
| 4 |  |  |
| 5 |  |  |
| 6 |  |  |
| 7 |  |  |
| 8 |  |  |

### Additional Notes
(surprises, problems, solutions, etc.)

Name: _____ Date: _____

**Directions:** After three weeks (or other determined time) of observing your new crystal grow, remove it from the solution and setup you created. Measure it and record the results. Then, answer the questions.

**Length of Crystal at the Longest Point:** _____

### Photo or Sketch of Your Crystal

1. How long was your crystal growing? _____

2. Was your procedure to grow a sugar crystal successful? What is your evidence?

   _____

   _____

3. Does your sugar crystal look like candy people would want to eat? Why or why not?

   _____

   _____

   _____

Name: _____ Date: _____

**Directions:** Answer the questions to reflect on your sugar crystals.

1. What problems did you face and how did you handle them?

_____

_____

_____

2. What about this challenge are you most proud of?

_____

_____

3. What advice would you give to someone who wants to grow their own sugar crystals?

_____

_____

4. Draw a picture of yourself and your team during a part of this challenge. Write a caption.

# Ocean Currents Teaching Support

## Overview of Unit Activities

Students will learn about and explore oceanic circulation through the following activities:

- reading about ocean currents
- reading about effects of melting glaciers and sea ice
- observing the sinking movement of cold water
- creating educational posters
- analyzing a pie chart showing data on ocean trash
- creating cargo boats

## Materials Per Group

### Week 1

- basic school supplies
- clear container filled with room temperature (or slightly warm) water
- food coloring

- freezer
- ice cube tray
- posterboard
- water

### STEAM Challenge

- basic school supplies
- craft sticks (6–10)
- duct tape
- foam cups (4–6)
- foil
- large container filled with water (the size will determine the maximum boat size students can make)
- masking tape
- modeling clay

- pennies (500; other coins or washers also work)
- pipe cleaners (5–10)
- plastic bags (2)
- plastic wrap
- shower cap
- small balloons (3–4)
- straws (10–15)
- string (3–4 feet, 1 m)
- wax paper

## Setup and Instructional Tips

- **Week 1 Day 3:** You may choose to prepare ice cubes ahead of time to save time.
- **STEAM Challenge:** The challenge can be done individually or in groups.  Students working in groups should sketch their own designs first.  Then, have them share designs in groups and choose one together.

## Discussion Questions

- What can we do to reduce ocean pollution, such as litter, and to convince folks to use less plastic?
- What happens to the movement of water as it warms and cools?
- How did people of the past and people of today rely on ocean currents?
- How does the ocean interact with the atmosphere?

## Additional Notes

- **Possible Misconception:** Oceans do not impact weather.
  **Truth:** Ocean currents and sea-surface temperatures play an enormous role in weather climate.

## Scaffolding and Extension Suggestions

- Support students with material ideas by encouraging them to start by testing materials to see what sinks or floats.
- Give students a budget, and have them spend their pretend money to buy the materials. This will reduce student waste of materials while teaching them about the realistic aspect of budget constraints.

## Answer Key

**Week 1 Day 1**
1. B
2. D

**Week 1 Day 2**
1. on land
2. the North and South Poles
3. Australia
4. Sea levels rising which causes flooding. Weather patterns are changing with some areas seeing more storms and others experiencing drought. Certain animals may go extinct.
5. Answers should include students' ideas for how they can help.

**Week 1 Day 5**
1. plastic pieces—especially plastic bags
2. 8%
3. That would not make sense as a priority because paper grocery bags do not even appear on this chart as something they collected.
4. Students will likely pick C because plastic pieces/plastic bags constituted the largest percentage of what was collected. Accept all answers with reasoned arguments.

**Weeks 2 & 3**
See STEAM Challenge Rubric on page 221.

**Day 1**

Name: _____ Date: _____

**Directions:** Read the text, and choose the best answer for each question.

Ocean water moves in continuous and predictable ways. These movements are known as ocean currents.

Ocean currents are caused by different forces:

- wind—affects surface currents more than deep water currents
- the Coriolis Effect—affects currents due to the spinning of Earth
- temperature—cold water tends to sink below warmer water
- salinity—saltier water tends to sink below less salty water

Knowing which way ocean currents move is important in many ways. For example, ships can reduce how much fuel they use by planning their trip to have the currents move them along as much as possible. Traveling against currents requires more energy. Some countries are looking into harnessing the power of ocean currents to generate electricity. Understanding currents can tell us where to find certain fish. Cold water currents tend to bring more plankton to an area. Fish often cluster in those areas.

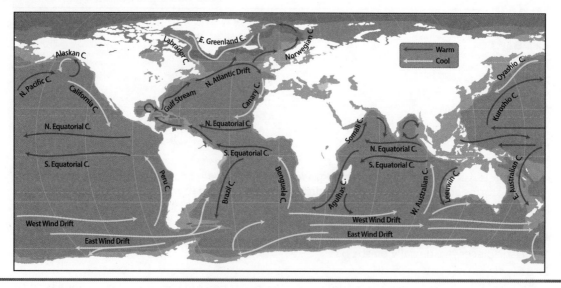

1. According to the map, which coast of South America is likely to have colder water?

   Ⓐ East coast        Ⓑ West coast

2. All of the following contribute to how ocean currents flow EXCEPT:

   Ⓐ how salty the water is        Ⓓ depth of the oceans

   Ⓑ water temperature            Ⓔ wind

   Ⓒ spinning of Earth

**Name:** _____ **Date:** _____

**Directions:** Read the text, and study the pictures. Then, answer the questions.

Glaciers are thickly packed ice that formed on land. They are so heavy that their own weight causes them to constantly move, even if only slowly. Ninety-nine percent of Earth's glaciers are at Earth's north and south poles. However, every continent except Australia has some glaciers. The water frozen in glaciers is freshwater.

Over the last century, many of the world's glaciers have been melting. When we burn fossil fuels to make electricity, heat, and for transportation, we release greenhouse gases. This causes Earth's temperature to rise and melts glaciers.

As glaciers melt into the ocean, they cause the ocean levels to rise. This is already causing flooding in many areas around the world. The melted glaciers also affect ocean currents, which changes weather. Some places are seeing more and more dangerous storms. Others are experiencing drought. Some animals, such as walruses, polar bears, and penguins, depend on glaciers and sea ice. As their homes disappear, those animals may disappear with them.

1. Where do glaciers form? _____

2. Where are most glaciers found? _____

3. Which continent does NOT have glaciers? _____

4. What are some problems created by melting glaciers and sea ice?

_____

_____

5. What are some things you can do to help with the problem?

_____

_____

**Name:** _____ **Date:** _____

**Directions:** One thing that affects ocean currents is water temperature. Follow the steps to see how water of different temperatures interact.

> **Question:** How do warm and cold water interact?

> **Materials**
>
> clear container filled with room temperature water
> food coloring    freezer    ice cube tray    water

### Steps

1. Dye some water and freeze it into ice cubes. Use enough dye that you get a vibrant color, making it easier to see in this activity.

2. Drop a colored ice cube into the clear container of water.

3. Observe what happens to the cold, colored water as the ice melts. Draw your observations. Then, describe them in words.

_____

_____

_____

 **Talk About It!**

What do you think would happen if fresh water melted into salt water?

Name: _____ Date: _____

**Directions:** Research an issue relating to our oceans that is interesting to you, and create a slide presentation or poster to educate others about it.

---

**Possible Topics**

- how the melting of glaciers affects the oceans and sea life
- your favorite sea animal and how it is being affected by global warming
- Great Pacific Garbage Patch—what is it and why should we be concerned about it?
- storm drains and storm water runoff—what is it and why do we need to know about it?
- ocean currents—what are they and how do they affect the weather?

---

### Presentation Tips

Make your presentation or poster look interesting and engaging so people choose to pay attention and read it. Look at images of posters and slides online to get ideas of what is eye-catching and interesting to read. Here are some other tips:

- Do not use too many words—use images to help make your point.
- To drive home your point, have only one message per poster or slide.
- Everything should be clear and easy to understand.

**Day 5**

Name: _____ Date: _____

**Directions:** Read the text, and study the graph.  Then, answer the questions.

Some communities do surveys when they pick up trash from the beach or water, then examine what they collect.  Shown here is a graph, by percentage, of what kind of trash one community found on their beaches and in the waters nearby.  They collected the data for a year.

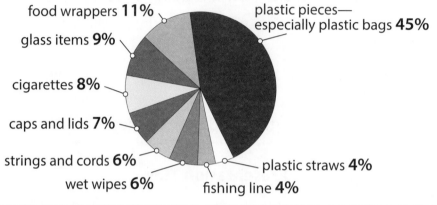

food wrappers **11%**
glass items **9%**
cigarettes **8%**
caps and lids **7%**
strings and cords **6%**
wet wipes **6%**
plastic pieces—
especially plastic bags **45%**
plastic straws **4%**
fishing line **4%**

**1.** According to this graph, what type of garbage did they collect the most of?

_____

**2.** What percentage of garbage collected was cigarettes? _____

**3.** Would it make sense for the town to prioritize reducing how many paper grocery bags they use?  Explain your reasoning.

_____

_____

**4.** Imagine you were going to make the case for a law to be passed in the town. Which of these laws do you think would be best to reduce the most trash at this beach?

    (A)  No smoking at the beach.

    (B)  Only permit drink containers that have lids or caps that stay attached.

    (C)  Ban distributing free plastic bags on or near the beach.

Explain your choice.

_____

_____

Name: _____ Date: _____

**Directions:** Read the text. Record the challenge criteria and constraints in the chart. Summarize the challenge in your own words. Then, write any questions you need answered before you begin the challenge.

## The Challenge

Much of what we have learned about the oceans has been because of the invention of boats. As we have learned more about oceans, that in turn has affected how we build boats. For example, knowing that boats float higher in salt water than in fresh water helps people load ships properly, so they are less likely to sink.

Your challenge is to build a cargo boat that holds as much weight as possible. You will float your boat in a large container of fresh water and add weight in the form of coins. You can add coins until the boat tips over or sinks. Your boat must be smaller than the water container so that it fits in the container for the test. Your teacher will let you know the dimensions of the container. You may use the materials provided to you.

| Criteria for a Successful Cargo Boat | Constraints |
|---|---|
|  |  |
|  |  |
|  |  |

*Note: Your teacher may have additional constraints, such as time limits. You may add criteria if you choose to set additional goals.

### My Summary

_____

_____

### My Questions

_____

_____

Name: _____ Date: _____

**Directions:** Conduct additional research about boat designs. Answer the questions. Think about which materials would work best, and record your ideas in the chart. Then, brainstorm and record other notes or ideas for your design. Discuss ideas with others, and add to your brainstorming.

1. What is similar about the boat designs you found during your research?

   _____

   _____

2. What is different about the boat designs?

   _____

   _____

3. What materials are boats, such as cargo boats, made of?

   _____

| Material | How It Might Help My Cargo Boat Design |
|---|---|
|  |  |
|  |  |
|  |  |
|  |  |
|  |  |
|  |  |

**My Cargo Boat Brainstorming**

**Name:** _____ **Date:** _____

**Directions:** Sketch two or more designs for your cargo boat. Try to sketch some design options that are very different from each other. Label the parts and materials. Circle the design you think will work best. Or circle the ideas you will combine from multiple designs. Then, answer the question.

1. What concerns do you have about your design?

_____

_____

## Unit 10: Ocean Currents

Name: _____ Date: _____

**Directions:** Plan the tools and materials you will need. Plan your steps. Then, gather your materials, and build your cargo boat. Record notes as you build.

### Tools and Materials

| Item Needed | Amount Needed | Item Needed | Amount Needed |
|---|---|---|---|
|  |  |  |  |
|  |  |  |  |
|  |  |  |  |

### Cargo Boat Building Plan

|  | Job, Task, or Role | Group Member(s) |
|---|---|---|
| 1 |  |  |
| 2 |  |  |
| 3 |  |  |
| 4 |  |  |
| 5 |  |  |
| 6 |  |  |
| 7 |  |  |
| 8 |  |  |

### Additional Notes
(surprises, problems, solutions, etc.)

**Name:** _____ **Date:** _____

**Directions:** Follow the directions to set up your test. Test your cargo boat and record the results. Then, answer the questions.

> Float your boat in a container of water. Add coins to the boat. You may put the coins anywhere on your boat. You may want to add a few coins at a time at first. Keep adding coins until the boat tips over or sinks. Count how many coins you used.

**Total Number of Coins My Boat Held:** _____

1. Was your design successful? What is your evidence?

   _____

   _____

   _____

2. What did you notice and learn from observing other groups' boats?

   _____

   _____

   _____

   _____

   _____

   _____

   _____

Name: _____ Date: _____

**Directions:** Reflect on your design, and answer the questions. Then, plan how you will improve it. Conduct additional research if needed.

1. What about your cargo boat design worked well?

   _____

   _____

   _____

2. What aspects did not work well or could be improved?

   _____

   _____

   _____

Draw a star next to one or more ways you will improve your design.

- My first design did not meet all the criteria because

  _____

  To improve it, I will _____

  _____

- Have the boat hold more weight.
- Add a company design to your boat.
- Use fewer materials.
- My own idea: _____

  _____

**Day 2**

Name: _____ Date: _____

**Directions:** Plan your new cargo boat design. Then, sketch a few new designs. Label the parts and materials. Mark what is new or different, and circle the design you think will work best. Then, complete the sentence.

**In my redesign, I will...**

add _____

remove _____

change _____

**1.** My new design will work better because _____

_____

_____

## Unit 10: Ocean Currents

Name: _____ Date: _____

**Directions:** Plan the tools and materials you will need. Plan your steps. Then, gather your materials, and rebuild your cargo boat.

### Tools and Materials

| Item Needed | Amount Needed | Item Needed | Amount Needed |
|---|---|---|---|
|  |  |  |  |
|  |  |  |  |
|  |  |  |  |

### Cargo Boat Rebuilding Plan

|  | Job, Task, or Role | Group Member(s) |
|---|---|---|
| 1 |  |  |
| 2 |  |  |
| 3 |  |  |
| 4 |  |  |
| 5 |  |  |
| 6 |  |  |
| 7 |  |  |
| 8 |  |  |

### Additional Notes
(surprises, problems, solutions, etc.)

Day 4

**Name:** _____ **Date:** _____

**Directions:** Follow the directions to set up your test. Retest your cargo boat and record the results. Then, answer the questions.

> Float your boat in a container of water. Add coins to the boat. You may put the coins anywhere on your boat. You may want to add a few coins at a time at first. Keep adding coins until the boat tips over or sinks. Count how many coins you used.

**Total Number of Coins My Boat Held:** _____

**1.** Was your new design successful? Explain your evidence.

_____

_____

_____

_____

**2.** Did your new design work better than your first? Explain your evidence.

_____

_____

_____

_____

Name: _____ Date: _____

**Directions:** Complete the table with pictures and/or words to reflect on the work you did during this challenge.

| Our Final Design | Questions I Still Have |
|---|---|
| | |
| **Problems Encountered** | **What I Learned** |
| | |
| **How I Contributed to the Group Design** | **My Favorite Part of Our Design** |
| | |

# Plate Tectonics Teaching Support

## Overview of Unit Activities

Students will learn about and explore plate tectonics through the following activities:

- reading about the theory of plate tectonics
- reading about and studying pictures of the effects of plate movements
- piecing together Earth's plates
- creating models of Earth's layers
- analyzing data and mapping major earthquakes
- creating vertical evacuation areas for tsunamis

## Materials Per Group

### Week 1

- basic school supplies
- construction paper
- foam hemisphere

- paint (water-based or acrylic)
- toothpicks

### STEAM Challenge

- basic school supplies
- foil
- index cards (5–10)
- large pan with high sides
- modeling clay
- plastic wrap

- sand (one bag)
- straws (10–15)
- sugar cubes (10)
- washers (2–3)
- water to fill pan
- toothpicks (15–20)

## Setup and Instructional Tips

- **Testing Days:** Testing may result in water on floors and tables. Prepare for this as needed.
- **STEAM Challenge:** The challenge can be done individually or in groups. Students working in groups should sketch their own designs first. Then, have them share designs in groups and choose one together.

## Discussion Questions

- Why do you think people live in areas that are likely to have more earthquakes or tsunamis? Why don't they move to a place that does not have so many?
- How might people have explained earthquakes and tsunamis long ago?
- How can people prepare for earthquakes and tsunamis?
- How have Earth's plates changed over time?
- What evidence is there of Earth's moving plates?

## Additional Notes

- **Possible Misconception:** Tsunamis are always very tall waves.
  **Truth:** Most tsunamis are less than 10 feet (3 m) high when they reach land. Tsunamis are dangerous because of their speed and volume.

## Scaffolding and Extension Suggestions

- Support students as needed by offering lower-level criteria, such as holding fewer sugar cubes or creating smaller "tsunamis" during testing.
- Encourage students to research recent tsunamis and the damage they caused.

## Answer Key

**Week 1 Day 1**
1. D
2. D

**Week 1 Day 2**
1. Two plates are moving toward each other; when plates collide, they sometimes cause the compressed land between them to move up and form mountains.
2. Plate movements can cause earthquakes. Sometimes a plate is pushed upward. This displaces ocean water and sends energy in waves toward land.

**Week 1 Day 5**
1. Earthquakes are located on the borders between tectonic plates. That is because people are living above where plates are sliding past each other or colliding or separating. They feel this plate tectonic movement in the form of earthquakes.

**Weeks 2 & 3**
See STEAM Challenge Rubric on page 221.

Name: _____ Date: _____

**Directions:** Read the text, and choose the best answer for each question.

We now know that the continents move. But it was not always known. A famous scientist, named Alfred Wegener, suggested that it was because the continents used to be one big continent that broke apart.

Evidence supported this theory. Some of the plant and animal fossils found along the coasts of the matching jigsaw puzzle pieces were the same. Also, matching rock layers were found on each coast, suggesting the rocks broke away from each other.

Eventually, scientists came to agree that the continents were once one big landmass. We call that original big piece Pangaea. Earth's surface is broken into about 20 pieces. Both the land and the oceans sit on top of these pieces. The pieces are called tectonic plates.

Permian period
225 million years ago

Triassic period
200 million years ago

Jurassic period
150 million years ago

Cretaceous period
65 million years ago

Present day

1. Which scientist first proposed that the continents were once all joined together?
   (A) Albert Einstein
   (B) Ellen Ochoa
   (C) George Washington Carver
   (D) Alfred Wegener

2. What evidence supports the hypothesis that the continents were once connected?
   (A) People can see the continents moving with their own eyes.
   (B) Some fossils in South America were the same as fossils in Africa.
   (C) Some rock layers in South America were identical to rock layers in Africa.
   (D) B and C
   (E) A and C

**Day 2**

Name: _____ Date: _____

**Directions:** Read the text, and study the picture. Then, answer the questions.

It is very hot beneath Earth's crust—hot enough that even solid rock flows. As rocks heat up, they rise. As they rise toward Earth's crust, they cool and then start to sink again. This causes convection currents in the mantle. The mantle is the layer of Earth below the crust. As these currents move, they cause the plates above them to move.

Tectonic plates move in different directions. Some are moving toward each other. This can cause mountains to form. Some plates are moving away from each other, which can cause valleys to form. In other cases, two plates are sliding past each other.

When tectonic plates move, we sometimes feel it in the form of earthquakes. The energy spreads as a wave. The waves may cause the ground to shake back and forth, move up and down, or move in a circular motion. Earthquakes in the ocean can cause tsunamis. When a plate is pushed upward, it displaces a large amount of water. The energy travels in waves across the ocean until it reaches land.

Volcanoes tend to erupt along plate boundaries too. This is because there's an opening in Earth's crust where magma can get through to the surface. Volcanoes are especially common where two plates are separating or where one plate is sliding under the other.

1. Mount Everest is the world's tallest mountain, and it is getting taller. It is located along a tectonic plate boundary. What is one explanation for how or why it continues to grow?

   _____

   _____

2. How can tectonic plate movement cause tsunamis?

   _____

   _____

**Name:** _____  **Date:** _____

**Directions:** Trace the tectonic plate pieces onto a separate sheet of paper. Label the traced pieces, cut them out, and glue them together on a sheet of construction paper. Note: The Pacific Plate is in two pieces to show the plates of a sphere on a flat surface.

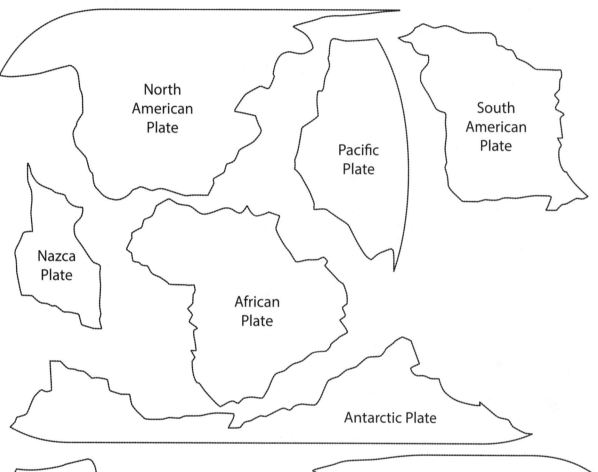

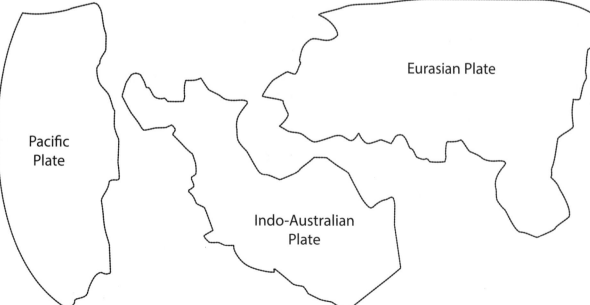

## Unit 11: Plate Tectonics

Name: _____ Date: _____

**Directions:** To understand the theory of plate tectonics, it helps to know the structure of the interior of Earth. Study the diagram. Then, use a foam hemisphere to paint a model of Earth. Label the layers with toothpick flags. Then, draw or paint the outlines of the major tectonic plates on one half of the surface of Earth.

**Structure of the Earth**

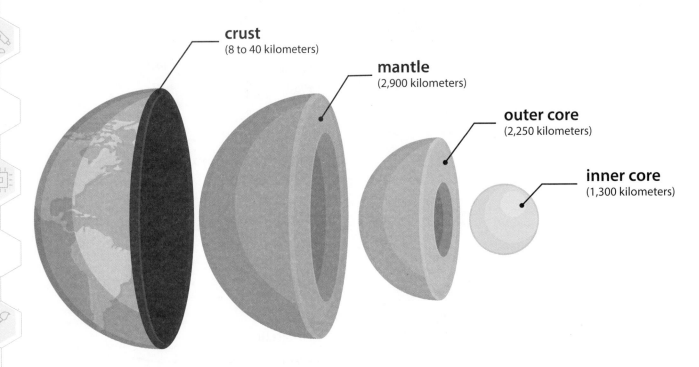

**crust**
(8 to 40 kilometers)

**mantle**
(2,900 kilometers)

**outer core**
(2,250 kilometers)

**inner core**
(1,300 kilometers)

 **Try This!**

Try to make the layers proportional to their thickness relative to the other layers. For example, the mantle should be the thickest layer. Add a flag to show where you live.

Name: _____ Date: _____

**Directions:** Read the text, and complete the task. Then, answer the questions.

Mapping the world's tectonic plates allows us to better understand why earthquakes are more likely in some areas than others. This helps us predict where future earthquakes are most likely to occur. The table shows the cities with some of the world's major recorded earthquakes.

**Task:** Mark the locations on the map of tectonic plates. Use another map to help you. The first one is done for you.

| Year | Location |
|------|----------|
| 1960 | Valdivia, Chile |
| 1906 | San Francisco, California, USA |
| 2011 | Under the ocean close to Sendai, Japan |
| 1964 | Near Anchorage, Alaska, USA |
| 2004 | Under the ocean, close to Sumatra, Indonesia |
| 2010 | Near Port-au-Prince, Haiti |

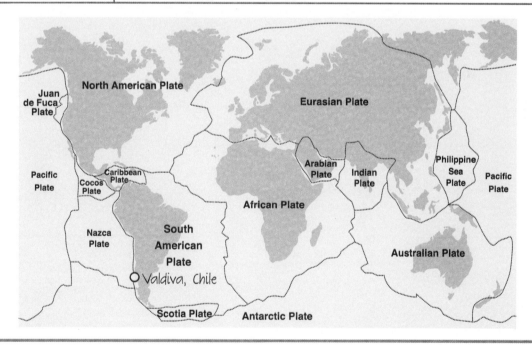

**1.** What conclusions can you make about the locations of major earthquakes?

_____

_____

_____

Name: _____ Date: _____

**Directions:** Sketch two or more designs for your vertical evacuation structure. Label the parts and materials. Where appropriate, make note of the purpose for each part. Circle the design you think will work best. Or, circle the ideas you will combine from multiple designs. Then, answer the question.

**1.** What concerns do you have about your design?

_____

_____

**Name:** _____ **Date:** _____

**Directions:** Research ways engineers design structures to withstand flooding and shaking. Your design is a vertical evacuation, so also research ways engineers build tall structures. Record some of your findings with words and pictures of example structures. Then, brainstorm and record other notes, ideas, or questions for your design. Discuss ideas with others, and add to your brainstorming.

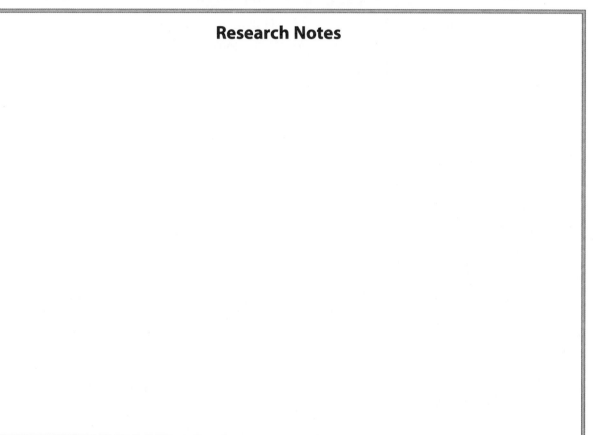

**Research Notes**

**My Vertical Evacuation Brainstorming**

Name: _____ Date: _____

**Directions:** Read the text. Record the challenge criteria and constraints in the chart. Summarize the challenge in your own words. Then, write any questions you need answered before you begin the challenge.

# The Challenge

Understanding earthquakes and tsunamis helps engineers find better ways to build structures that can withstand events. They study the local area to learn about the specific needs. Engineers also study materials, shapes, and features that help buildings to withstand these events. For example, sometimes designing ways for water to move past or through buildings can prevent flood waters from knocking down or carrying buildings away.

Your challenge is to build a vertical evacuation area for a community that could be hit by tsunamis. Instead of attempting to flee an area, residents can climb the structure to safety. You will place your structure on a pile of sand and simulate a tsunami. Your structure must withstand the force of the water. It must have room for and support five sugar cubes (people) and keep them dry. The base must fit on the sandy area you will create in one half of a large pan. You will simulate the water movement in a tsunami by lifting the end 1 inch (2.5 cm) high and dropping it.

| Criteria for a Successful Vertical Evacuation Structure | Constraints |
|---|---|
|  |  |
|  |  |
|  |  |

*Note: Your teacher may have additional constraints, such as time limits. You may add criteria if you choose to set additional goals.

## My Summary

_____

_____

## My Questions

_____

_____

**Day 1**

Name: _____ Date: _____

**Directions:** Reflect on your design, and answer the questions. Then, plan how you will improve it. Conduct additional research if needed.

**1.** What about your vertical evacuation structure worked well?

_____

_____

_____

**2.** What flaws were revealed during testing?

_____

_____

_____

**3.** What design ideas did you see from others that you might want to try?

_____

_____

_____

Draw a star next to one or more ways you will improve your design.

- My first design did not meet all the criteria because

_____

_____

To improve it, I will _____

- Make it support 10 sugar cubes and keep them dry.
- Include a way for people to get up to and down from the evacuation area.
- My own idea: _____

_____

Name: _____ Date: _____

**Directions:** Set up your test as shown in the diagram. Place your structure on the sand. Place five sugar cubes on or in your structure. Test your vertical evacuation structure by lifting the opposite end 1 inch (2.5 cm) high and dropping it. (If that did not create enough water to cover the sand, try lifting the end higher). Record the results. Then, answer the questions.

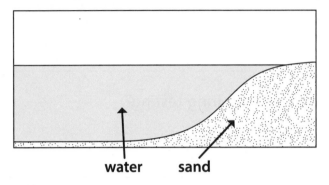

water      sand

1. Draw what your structure looked like after the water settled.

2. Did your structure remain standing and intact?     yes      no

3. Did your sugar cubes remain dry and on the structure?   yes      no

4. What did you notice happened to the sand as a result of the tsunami?

_____

_____

5. Was your vertical evacuation structure design a success? Explain your evidence.

_____

_____

_____

**Name:** _____ **Date:** _____

**Directions:** Plan the tools and materials you will need.  Plan your steps.  Then, gather your materials, and build your vertical evacuation structure.  Record notes as you build.

### Tools and Materials

| Item Needed | Amount Needed | Item Needed | Amount Needed |
|---|---|---|---|
| | | | |
| | | | |
| | | | |

### Vertical Evacuation Structure Building Plan

| | Job, Task, or Role | Group Member(s) |
|---|---|---|
| 1 | | |
| 2 | | |
| 3 | | |
| 4 | | |
| 5 | | |
| 6 | | |
| 7 | | |
| 8 | | |

### Additional Notes
(surprises, problems, solutions, etc.)

## Unit 11: Plate Tectonics

Name: _____  Date: _____

**Directions:** Plan your new vertical evacuation structure design. Then, sketch a few new designs. Label the parts and materials. Mark what is new or different, and circle the design you think will work best. Then, complete the sentence.

**In my redesign, I will...**

**add** _____

**remove** _____

**change** _____

**1.** My new design will work better because _____

_____

_____

Name: _____ Date: _____

**Directions:** Plan the tools and materials you will need. Plan your steps. Then, gather your materials, and rebuild your vertical evacuation structure.

### Tools and Materials

| Item Needed | Amount Needed | Item Needed | Amount Needed |
|---|---|---|---|
|  |  |  |  |
|  |  |  |  |
|  |  |  |  |

### Vertical Evacuation Structure Rebuilding Plan

|  | Job, Task, or Role | Group Member(s) |
|---|---|---|
| 1 |  |  |
| 2 |  |  |
| 3 |  |  |
| 4 |  |  |
| 5 |  |  |
| 6 |  |  |
| 7 |  |  |
| 8 |  |  |

### Additional Notes
(surprises, problems, solutions, etc.)

# The Water Cycle Teaching Support

## Overview of Unit Activities

Students will learn about and explore the water cycle through the following activities:

- reading about where water is on Earth
- reading about and studying pictures of the water cycle
- creating clouds in jars
- creating mini water cycles
- analyzing a graph of water usage
- creating water filtration systems

## Materials Per Group

### Week 1

- basic school supplies
- clear jar with lid
- hair spray
- hot water
- ice
- sealable plastic baggie

### STEAM Challenge

- basic school supplies
- dirt (handful)
- duct tape
- glass jars (2)
- hot water
- ice (handful)
- large and small containers that can hold boiling water (2)
- permanent markers in different colors
- plastic bottles (2)
- plastic wrap
- straws (4–5)
- tablespoon measuring spoon
- very hot water

## Setup and Instructional Tips

- **Safety Note:** Supervise students and use caution with boiling water. Use containers that can hold boiling water without shattering or melting.
- **STEAM Challenge:** The challenge can be done individually or in groups. Students working in groups should sketch their own designs first. Then, have them share designs in groups and choose one together.
- **Testing Days:** Testing should be done on sunny days. If this is not possible, you can simulate this using heat lamps. Ideally, students would test their water purifiers for one hour. If needed, you can reduce the amount of time, and should reduce the amount of water students will purify.

**Day 5**

**Name:** _____ **Date:** _____

**Directions:** Answer the questions to reflect on your vertical evacuation structure.

**1.** What was your favorite part of this challenge?

_____

_____

_____

**2.** Why is testing an important part of the engineering design process?

_____

_____

**3.** What did you learn from this challenge?

_____

_____

_____

_____

**4.** Would you want to be an engineer who designs structures to withstand events such as tsunamis?  Why or why not?

_____

_____

_____

**Day 4**

Name: _____ Date: _____

**Directions:** Set up your test the same way as before (see diagram). Place your new structure on the sand. Place 5–10 sugar cubes on or in your structure. Test your vertical evacuation structure by lifting the opposite end 1 inch (2.5 cm) high and dropping it. (If that did not create enough water to cover the sand, try lifting the end higher). Record the results. Then, answer the questions.

water     sand

1. Draw what your structure looked like after the water settled.

2. Did your structure remain standing and intact?          yes          no

3. Did your sugar cubes remain dry and on the structure?     yes          no

4. Did your new design work better? Explain your evidence.

_____

_____

_____

5. Do you think your design would hold up in a real tsunami? Why or why not?

_____

_____

**Name:** _____ **Date:** _____

**Directions:** Read the text, and study the diagram. Then, answer the questions.

Water on Earth moves a lot. It does not just move in flowing rivers. It also moves in other ways, such as when it evaporates or rains. As it moves, it may change from a solid to a liquid to a gas and back again. The movement of water on, through, and above Earth's surface is called the water cycle. Water moves through the water cycle in many ways. Here are some examples:

- Water evaporates from lakes, rivers, and the oceans.
- Some of it is suspended in the air. There is always some water in the air in the form of a gas called water vapor.
- Some water evaporates into clouds.
- Water may fall from clouds in the form of rain or snow.
- Some water may seep underground.
- Some water on the surface may flow back into rivers, lakes, and oceans.

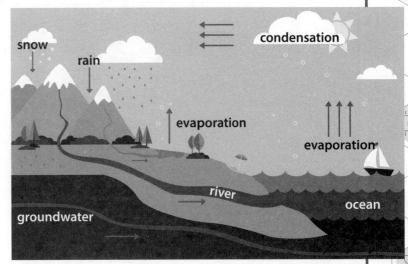

1. Describe the journey of a water droplet in a cloud as it moves through the water cycle and ends up back in a cloud.

_____

_____

_____

2. When water evaporates, it is changing from a liquid to a _____.

3. Why is the water cycle called a *cycle*?

_____

_____

Name: _____ Date: _____

**Directions:** Read the text, and choose the best answer for each question.

Earth is an unusual planet in that it has so much water. In fact, most of our planet is covered in water. Most of it is ocean water, which means it is salty. While many living things live in the oceans, humans cannot drink salt water to live. We need to drink fresh water, which is non-salty water. Less than three percent of the water on Earth is fresh water. Most of Earth's fresh water starts off as rain or snow. Some of it sinks into the ground and is called groundwater. Some fresh water collects in lakes or rivers. Most of the world's fresh water is frozen in ice sheets and glaciers near the North and South Poles.

**1.** Most of the water on the planet is found in _____.

- Ⓐ ice sheets and glaciers
- Ⓑ rivers and lakes
- Ⓒ ocean water
- Ⓓ groundwater

**2.** Most of the water on Earth is _____ water.

- Ⓐ ocean (salty) water
- Ⓑ fresh (non-salty) water

**3.** Where is most of the fresh water on Earth found?

- Ⓐ in the great lakes
- Ⓑ underground
- Ⓒ in the rain
- Ⓓ frozen near the North and South Poles

## Discussion Questions

- Why is water important to us?
- If there is always the same amount of water on Earth, then why is it important to conserve water?
- Should people be fined for not conserving enough water?  Why or why not?
- What makes some water unsafe to drink?  What are some ways people get safe water around the world?

## Additional Notes

- **Possible Misconception:** Ocean water can be drinking water in an emergency.
  **Truth:** The salt in ocean water will actually cause greater dehydration.
- **Possible Design Solutions:** The intention of the STEAM challenge is that students will use water evaporation and condensation to purify the water, in line with the unit.  A successful water purifier could be similar to this.  The empty cup in the center collects the clean condensation as it drips off the inside bottom of the plastic wrap.

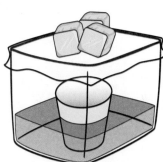

## Scaffolding and Extension Suggestions

- Show students videos of distillation and explain what is happening. This should help students to understand how they can apply these concepts to their water purifiers.
- Encourage students to add salt to their "dirty" water and see if they can successfully turn it into fresh water.

## Answer Key

**Week 1 Day 1**
1. C
2. A

3. D

**Week 1 Day 2**
1. Answers may vary but may include that the droplet rains down and evaporates back into the air and then re-condenses as part of a cloud.
2. gas (water vapor also acceptable)
3. Water is going round and round from sky to ground.  It keeps recycling.

**Week 1 Day 5**
1. 20%
2. 20%
3. faucet
4. 25 gallons
5. Examples: drinking water, brushing teeth, washing hands, hand washing dishes, or washing or caring for a pet

**Weeks 2 & 3**
See STEAM Challenge Rubric on page 221.

Name: _____ Date: _____

**Directions:** Read all the text through once.  Then, follow the steps to make a cloud in a jar.

Clouds form when water in the air condenses (turns back into a liquid) in the sky.  The water condenses in the cold air.  It also condenses onto something, such as dust or pollen.  In this activity, the hot water represents evaporating water.  The hair spray represents dust or pollen.  The ice represents the cold temperatures in the sky where clouds form.

## Materials

| clear jar with lid | hot water |
|---|---|
| hair spray | ice |

### Steps

1. Remove the lid.  Fill the jar one-third full of hot water.

2. Spray the inside of the jar with hair spray. One squirt will do.

3. Put the lid upside down on the jar.

4. Fill the lid with ice.

5. Watch the cloud form inside the jar!

6. If you wish, remove the lid and watch the cloud escape.

7. Draw what you observed.

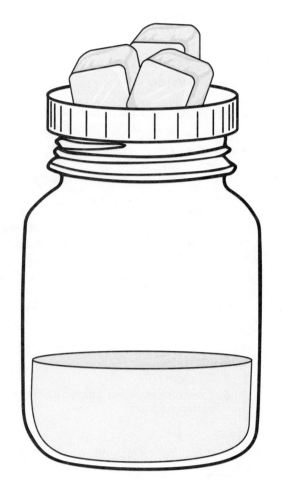

Name: _____ Date: _____

**Directions:** Follow the steps to create your own water cycle in a bag.

### Steps

1. On a sealable plastic bag, use permanent markers to draw a water cycle. Draw some land, but also keep some areas clear for where the water will go. Draw and label as many parts of the water cycle as you can.

2. Fill the bag partly with water to represent the oceans, groundwater, lakes, etc.

3. Show your bag to someone and explain how it is illustrating the water cycle.

4. Tape the bag to a sunny window and see if some water evaporates, forming a mini water cycle in the bag! If you wish, you can tape the bag at a slight angle to mimic water running off the land into a lake, river, or ocean.

This is a simple version. Add more details to yours.

## Unit 12: The Water Cycle

Name: _____ Date: _____

**Directions:** Conduct additional research about water purifiers as needed. Answer the question. Think about which materials would work best, and record your ideas in the chart. Then, brainstorm and record other notes or ideas for your design. Discuss ideas with others, and add to your brainstorming.

1. How do people use heat, evaporation, and condensation to purify water?

_____

_____

_____

| Material | How It Might Help My Water Purifier Design |
|---|---|
|  |  |
|  |  |
|  |  |
|  |  |
|  |  |
|  |  |

**My Water Purifier Brainstorming**

 **Think About It!**

Where will the clean water collect?

Name: _____ Date: _____

**Directions:** Read the text. Record the challenge criteria and constraints in the chart. Summarize the challenge in your own words. Then, write any questions you need answered before you begin the challenge.

## The Challenge

Around the world, people purify water for drinking. They may wish to kill dangerous microbes, remove dirt, and/or remove salt from the water.

In this challenge, you will build a water purifier modeled after the water cycle. It will purify water containing dirt. You will be given a half gallon of muddy, dark brown or black water. From this water, your goal is to produce a tablespoon (15 mL) of clear water. You will have succeeded if the water you produce is transparent. You may use the materials provided to you, such as bowls, cups, plastic wrap, and ice. You may only use heat (from the sun, a heat lamp, and/or from boiling water) as your energy source. Making use of gravity is acceptable. You have one hour for your water purifier to produce a tablespoon full of purified water.

| Criteria for a Successful Water Purifier | Constraints |
|---|---|
| | |
| | |
| | |

*Note: Your teacher may have additional constraints, such as time limits. You may add criteria if you choose to set additional goals.

### My Summary

_____

_____

### My Questions

_____

_____

Name: _____  Date: _____

**Directions:** Below is a graph of the Williams Family daily home water use. Study the graph, and answer the questions.

1. A pie chart should add up to 100 percent to show the total usage. What percent should be in the section labeled other? _____

2. What percentage of their daily water use is spent on showers? _____

3. What requires the least amount of water in their day? _____

4. If they use 100 gallons of water per day, then how many gallons do they use flushing the toilet? _____

5. What types of water usage do you think might be included in "other"?

_____

6. What types of activities do you think might be included in "faucet"?

_____

**Name:** _____ **Date:** _____

**Directions:** Put a half gallon of water in a container. Add dirt to it until it is dark brown or black in color. Place your water purifier in the location you have planned (e.g., outdoors, under a heat lamp). After one hour, measure and record the results. Then, answer the questions.

1. Observe your water purifier during and at the end of the one hour. Draw what you observed and/or describe it in words.

2. How much purified water did your design collect after one hour?

   _____

3. Based on these results, would you consider your water purifier successful? Explain your evidence.

   _____

   _____

   _____

## Unit 12: The Water Cycle

Name: _____ Date: _____

**Directions:** Plan the tools and materials you will need. Plan your steps. Then, gather your materials, and build your water purifier. Record notes as you build.

### Tools and Materials

| Item Needed | Amount Needed | Item Needed | Amount Needed |
|---|---|---|---|
|  |  |  |  |
|  |  |  |  |
|  |  |  |  |

### Water Purifier Building Plan

| | Job, Task, or Role | Group Member(s) |
|---|---|---|
| 1 |  |  |
| 2 |  |  |
| 3 |  |  |
| 4 |  |  |
| 5 |  |  |
| 6 |  |  |
| 7 |  |  |
| 8 |  |  |

### Additional Notes
(problems, solutions, successes, etc.)

**Name:** _____ **Date:** _____

**Directions:** Sketch two or more designs for your water purifier. Label the parts and materials. Where appropriate, make note of the purpose for each part. Circle the design you think will work best. Or circle the ideas you will combine from multiple designs. Then, answer the question.

1. What concerns do you have about your design?

_____

_____

## Unit 12: The Water Cycle

Name: _____ Date: _____

**Directions:** Reflect on your water purifier design. Answer the questions. Then, plan how you will improve it. Conduct additional research if needed.

1. What about your water purifier worked well?

   _____

   _____

   _____

2. What aspects did not work well or could be improved?

   _____

   _____

   _____

Draw a star next to one or more ways you will improve your design.

- My first design did not meet all the criteria because

  _____

  To improve it, I will _____

  _____

- I will make it more efficient and purify more water. My goal is to purify

  _____ of water.

- I will make the design easier to transport, so that campers or hikers can easily carry it.

- My own idea: _____

  _____

**Name:** _____ **Date:** _____

**Directions:** Plan your new water purifier design. Then, sketch a few new designs. Label the parts and materials. Mark what is new or different, and circle the design you think will work best. Then, complete the sentence.

**In my redesign, I will…**

**add** _____

**remove** _____

**change** _____

**1.** My new design will work better because _____

_____

_____

Name: _____ Date: _____

**Directions:** Complete the table with pictures and/or words to reflect on the work you did during this challenge.

| Our Final Design | What I Am Most Proud Of |
|---|---|
| | |
| **Problems Encountered** | **What I Learned** |
| | |
| **How We Solved Problems** | **What I Would Do Differently** |
| | |

Name: _____ Date: _____

**Directions:** Repeat the steps to set up your test. Test your redesigned water purifier, and measure and record the results. Then, answer the questions.

1. Observe your water purifier during and at the end of the one hour. Draw what you observed and/or describe it in words.

2. How much purified water did your design collect after one hour?

_____

3. Did your new design perform better? Explain your evidence.

_____

_____

_____

4. Describe any other goals you set for your redesign, whether you achieved them, and what evidence you have.

_____

_____

_____

Name: _____ Date: _____

**Directions:** Plan the tools and materials you will need. Plan your steps. Then, gather your materials, and rebuild your water purifier.

## Tools and Materials

| Item Needed | Amount Needed | Item Needed | Amount Needed |
|---|---|---|---|
|  |  |  |  |
|  |  |  |  |
|  |  |  |  |

 **Quick Tip!**

It is okay to change jobs if group members want to try something different.

## Water Purifier Rebuilding Plan

| | Job, Task, or Role | Group Member(s) |
|---|---|---|
| 1 |  |  |
| 2 |  |  |
| 3 |  |  |
| 4 |  |  |
| 5 |  |  |
| 6 |  |  |
| 7 |  |  |
| 8 |  |  |

# Engineering Design Process

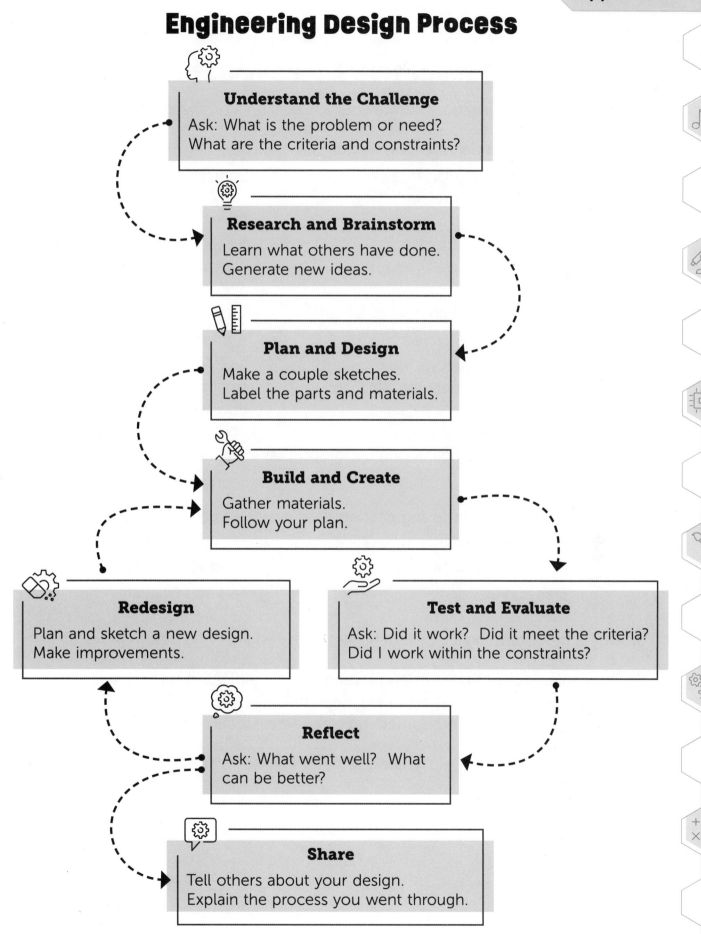

**Understand the Challenge**

Ask: What is the problem or need?
What are the criteria and constraints?

**Research and Brainstorm**

Learn what others have done.
Generate new ideas.

**Plan and Design**

Make a couple sketches.
Label the parts and materials.

**Build and Create**

Gather materials.
Follow your plan.

**Redesign**

Plan and sketch a new design.
Make improvements.

**Test and Evaluate**

Ask: Did it work? Did it meet the criteria?
Did I work within the constraints?

**Reflect**

Ask: What went well? What
can be better?

**Share**

Tell others about your design.
Explain the process you went through.

Name: _____  Date: _____

# Summative Assessment

**Directions:** Read the questions. Write your answers on a separate sheet of paper.

1. Which of these is a definition of *criteria*?

   (A) The list of materials that can be used in the project.

   (B) The goal of the project.

   (C) Something that is too small to be seen without a microscope.

   (D) A rule which tells you not to copy or plagiarize.

2. Which of these is a definition of *constraint*?

   (A) The goal of the project.

   (B) When someone says something is unacceptable.

   (C) A rule that limits or restricts.

   (D) Something that is too small to be seen without a microscope.

3. Why are parts of the engineering design process shown in graphics as a continuous circle?

4. During which parts of the engineering design process do you discover whether a design met the criteria?

   (A) Research and Brainstorm

   (B) Plan and Design

   (C) Build and Create

   (D) Test and Evaluate

5. Why is brainstorming an important part of the engineering design process?

6. Stephanie Kwolek, a chemist and inventor, once said, "All sorts of things can happen when you are open to new ideas and playing around with things." Do you think that sounds like something an engineer would say? Why or why not?

7. A friend asks for your help making something to sell at a craft expo. What would you do first?

Name: _____ Date: _____

# STEAM Challenge Rubric

**Directions:** Think about the challenge. Score each item on a scale of 3 to 1. Circle your score.

| | 3 | 2 | 1 |
|---|---|---|---|
| **Criteria** | The final design was successful in meeting the goals. Or major improvements were made through logical, evidence-based design changes. | The final design was partially successful in meeting the goals. Attempts to improve the design were partially successful. | The final project was not successful in meeting the goals. Attempts were not thoughtful or based on research. |
| **Constraints** | All instructions for the challenge were followed. The final design was completed within the constraints given. | Some instructions for the challenge were followed. The final design was partially completed within the constraints given. | Instructions for the challenge were not followed. No consideration for constraints were made. |
| **Group Collaboration** | Students cooperated to complete the project. Students divided work fairly. Students accepted and learned from each other's mistakes and worked together to find solutions. There was consistently calm communication. | Work was divided fairly among group members for the most part. Group members were sometimes supportive or helpful in problem-solving. Students struggled to compromise but found ways to work together. | Work was not divided fairly. Group members were not supportive of mistakes nor helpful in problem-solving. Heated disagreements occurred and/or compromises could not be reached. |
| **Creativity** | Students applied their knowledge in several unique ways to solve problems. New and innovative approaches to the problem were tested. | Students applied their knowledge in one unique way. At least one innovative approach to the problem was tested. | Students did not attempt any unique solutions to the problem. Innovative approaches were not tested. |

Student Score: _____     Teacher Score: _____

# Digital Resources

## Accessing the Digital Resources

The digital resources can be downloaded by following these steps:

1. Go to **www.tcmpub.com/digital**.

2. Use the ISBN number to redeem the digital resources.

   **ISBN: 978-1-0876-6210-7**

3. Respond to the question using the book.

4. Follow the prompts on the Content Cloud website to sign in or create a new account.

5. Choose the digital resources you would like to download. You can download all the files at once or a specific group of files.

## Contents of the Digital Resources

- Safety Contract
- Sentence frames to help guide friendly student feedback
- Materials requests for students' families
- Student Glossary
- Materials list for the whole book

## References Cited

Bybee, Rodger W. 2013. *The Case for STEM Education: Challenges and Opportunities.* Arlington, VA: NSTA Press.

NGSS Lead States. 2013. "Next Generation Science Standards: For States, By States APPENDIX I—Engineering Design in the NGSS." Washington, DC.